Dear People

Remembering Jonestown

Dear People

Remembering Jonestown

Edited by
Denice Stephenson

Selections from the
Peoples Temple Collection
at the California Historical Society

California Historical Society Press
San Francisco, California

Heyday Books
Berkeley, California

California Historical Society Press is a collaboration between the California Historical Society and Heyday Books. California Historical Society Press is supported by grants from The William Randolph Hearst Foundation and The Mericos Foundation. Thanks also to LEF Foundation for their generous support of this volume.

Heyday Books, founded in 1974, works to deepen people's understanding and appreciation of the cultural, artistic, historic, and natural resources of California and the American West. It operates under a 501(c)(3) nonprofit educational organization (Heyday Institute) and, in addition to publishing books, sponsors a wide range of programs, outreach, and events.

Library of Congress Cataloging-in-Publication Data
Dear people : remembering Jonestown / edited by Denice Stephenson.
    p. cm.
  Includes bibliographical references and index.
  ISBN 1-59714-002-3 (pbk. : alk. paper)
  1. Jonestown Mass Suicide, Jonestown, Guyana, 1978—Sources. 2. Peoples Temple—History—Sources. I. Stephenson, Denice.
  BP605.P46D44 2005
  289.9—dc22

                          2004030043

Cover photo ©Royalty-Free/CORBIS. Front inset: Jim Jones (in hat and sunglasses) with early settlers and construction crew of Peoples Temple Agricultural Mission in Guyana. Back inset: Peoples Temple member in Jonestown. Tommy Johnson, gardening supervisor. MSP 3800. Peoples Temple collection, California Historical Society
Cover design by Rebecca LeGates
Book design by Kathleen Szawiola
Printing and binding by: United Graphics, Inc., Mattoon, IL

Orders, inquiries, and correspondence should be addressed to:
Heyday Books
P. O. Box 9145, Berkeley, CA 94709
(510) 549-3564, Fax (510) 549-1889
www.heydaybooks.com

10   9   8   7   6   5   4   3   2   1

Contents

Part Three

Part Four

Part Five
The Day of Departure and Death   111

Part Six
A Community Lost   143

Foreword

Rare is the moment when an archival collection literally knocks the breath right out of you. At the California Historical Society, among the memorabilia, photographs, books, and records that compose one of the country's finest collections on the history of California and the West, is a long row of archival shelves. They are filled with neatly filed and stacked boxes recounting the lives, dreams, hopes, and aspirations, and the tragedy, of Peoples Temple, known to the world as "Jonestown." Merely knowing that this archive exists is fascinating; standing in front of the remaining record of such a compelling story can be numbing and sad; opening those boxes, we find the people of Peoples Temple—the faces of Jonestown.

The California Historical Society is honored and privileged to serve as the caretaker and steward of this important collection. With this book, respectfully assembled by Denice Stephenson, we catch a glimpse into the story behind the story, the depth of the human experience that was the heart of Peoples Temple. As a Californian, I clearly remember the horror of the news from San Francisco and Guyana during those ten days in November. It was an awful, sinking, bizarre experience, with the Jonestown deaths followed so closely by the assassinations of San Francisco Mayor George Moscone and gay rights activist and City Supervisor Harvey Milk. It reminded many of us of 1968 and the assassinations, one after another, Martin Luther King and Robert Kennedy. Had our world gone mad? What did this all mean?

Time gives us the opportunity to reflect on this question, to study, appreciate, and yes, celebrate the lives and dreams of the victims lost in Jonestown. We hope this book will help with that process, offering a glimpse of the stories which are available to us today because of the long and hard work of the many researchers, archivists, and librarians who have carefully stored and preserved this record of the lives and times of the people of Jonestown and the experiences of their families through a tragic period in California's story.

Stephen Becker
Executive Director
California Historical Society

Preface

When we remember Jonestown, we usually remember the deaths of Jim Jones and his followers in a jungle far away from the United States. We remember poison and Kool-Aid. We may remember they were members of a group from California called Peoples Temple and that many of them were African Americans. Some of us remember that a congressman and several journalists died. For the most part, we remember that a lot of people died. We do not remember—we may never have known—how they lived.

In *Dear People: Remembering Jonestown,* we take a look at the papers that were left behind by a group of people whose collective death has long overwhelmed their individual stories. Their papers give us an opportunity to learn more about Peoples Temple, who the members were, and what they thought about faith, politics, race relations, and social justice.

Dear People: Remembering Jonestown is based on a selection of documents and photographs from the Peoples Temple Collection at the California Historical Society and published in collaboration with Heyday Books. This unique and important collection contains more than one hundred and seventy boxes of letters, documents, photographs, and audiotapes. The contents of the collection span the fifty years since the founding of Peoples Temple and are sharply divided into two sections by the day of the deaths in Jonestown. The documents before the Jonestown tragedy reflect the energy of an organization and families on the move, on a search. They are filled with examples of complex ideologies and relationships, hard work and big dreams, and conflicts at all levels—between parents and children, members and leaders, husbands and wives, newspapers and readers, elected officials and constituents. After the deaths in Jonestown, the records are about a different type of search—a search for responsibility, for answers, for closure. These records are about the loss of a community, the burial of the dead, the disbursement of the community's assets, and the preservation of its records.

The Peoples Temple Collection also includes documents generated by U.S. government agencies in response to the tragedy in Jonestown. Agencies such as the Department of State, Department of Defense, Federal Bureau of Investigation, and Customs Service have released selections from their records under the Freedom of Information Act. The largest selection of these records consists of copies of Peoples Temple papers, found in Jonestown after the deaths, that were collected by American and Guyanese government officials and subsequently turned over to the FBI for its investigation of the murder of Congressman Leo J. Ryan.

We chose selections from this extensive collection that we thought provided an intimate glimpse of members' lives and helped us to narrate the history of Peoples Temple. We found our title, *Dear People,* in the salutations of letters addressed to Peoples Temple from the general public. We included excerpts from Jonestown survivor Hyacinth Thrash's book, *The Onliest One Alive,* and transcripts of Peoples Temple recordings from a website maintained by the Jonestown Institute, "Alternative Considerations of Jonestown and Peoples Temple." In several of the selections based on transcripts we found in the collection, we have corrected the spelling and punctuation. We also indicated when a selection is a part of a longer document. The images in the book, except where noted, are from the Peoples Temple Collection. Among the many books about Peoples Temple that guided us through its history are John R. Hall's *Gone from the Promised Land: Jonestown in American Cultural History,* Tim Reiterman's *Raven: The Untold Story of the Rev. Jim Jones and His People,* Mary McCormick Maaga's *Hearing the Voices of Jonestown,* and *Peoples Temple and Black Religion in America,* edited by Rebecca Moore, Anthony B. Pinn, and Mary R. Sawyer.

We are grateful to the staffs of the California Historical Society and Heyday Books for their support of this project. We thank the survivors of the Jonestown tragedy who have shared their memories and the researchers who have shared their questions.

We begin with a poem, a Jonestown resident's last letter, and a mother's plea.

from "I Come from the Nigger Yard"

Martin Carter / 1954

In May 1978, Jonestown residents drafted a booklet called *Questions and Answers about the Peoples Temple Agricultural Project* for the Guyanese public. They dedicated it "to the beautiful people of Guyana" and included this excerpt from Guyanese poet Martin Carter, "I Come from the Nigger Yard." Martin Carter (1927–1997) is considered one of Guyana's most important poets and also served as minister of information and culture.

I come from the nigger yard of yesterday
leaping from the oppressor's hate
and the scorn of myself.
I come to the world with scars upon my soul
wounds on my body, fury in my hands.
I turn to the histories of men, and the lives of the peoples
I examine the shower of sparks, the wealth of the dreams
I am pleased with the glories and sad with the sorrows
rich with the riches, poor with the loss.
From the nigger yard of yesterday I come with my burden.
To the world of tomorrow I turn with my strength.

"Last Words"

November 18, 1978

Amerian Embassy officials discovered this unsigned document, written as people were dying in Jonestown, among the papers that were gathered there after the deaths. A copy of the Guyanese notebook containing the letter was later turned over to the FBI and filed with financial papers from the agricultural project.

TO WHOMEVER FINDS THIS NOTE

Collect all the tapes, all the writing, all the history. The story of this movement, this action, must be examined over and over. It must be understood in all of its incredible dimensions. Words fail. We have pledged our lives to this great cause. We are proud to have something to die for. We do not fear death. We hope that the world will someday realize the ideals of brotherhood, justice and equality that Jim Jones has lived and died for. We have all chosen to die for this cause. We know there is no way that we can avoid misinterpretation. But Jim Jones and this movement were born too soon. The world was not ready to let us live.

I am sorry there is no eloquence as I write these final words. We are resolved, but grieved that we cannot make the truth of our witness clear.

This is the last day of our lives. May the world find a way to a new birth of social justice. If there is any way that our lives and the life of Jim Jones can ever help that take place, we will not have lived in vain.

Jim Jones did not order anyone to attack or kill anyone. It was done by individuals who had too much of seeing people try to destroy this movement [and] Jim Jones. Their actions have left us no alternative, and rather than see this cause decimated, we have chosen to give our lives. We are proud of that choice.

Please try to understand. Look at *all.* Look at all in perspective. Look at Jonestown, see what we have tried to do—This was a monument to *life,* to the [re]newal of the human spirit, broken by capitalism, by a system of exploitation & injustice. Look at all that was built by a beleaguered people. We did not want this kind of ending—we wanted to live, to shine, to bring light to a world that is dying for a little bit of love. To those left behind of our loved ones, many of whom will not understand, who never knew this truth, *grieve not,* we are grateful for this opportunity to bear witness—a bitter witness—history has chosen our destiny in spite of our own desire to forge our own. We were at a cross/purpose with history. But we are calm in this hour of our collective leave-taking. As I write these words people are silently amassed, taking a quick potion, inducing sleep, *relief.* We are a long-suffering people. Many of us are weary with a long search, a long struggle—going back not only in our lifetime, but a long painful heritage.

(*Please* see the histories of our people that are in a building called teachers resource center).

Many of us are now dead. Each moment, another passes over to a peace. We are begging only for some understanding. It will take more than small minds, reporters' minds, to fathom these events. Something must come of this. Beyond all the circumstances surrounding the immediate event, someone can perhaps find the symbolic, the eternal in this moment—the meaning of a people, a struggle—I wish I had time to put it all together, that I had done it. I did not do it. I failed to write the book. Someone else, others, will have to do this. Please study this movement, from the very origins of Jim Jones in the rural poverty of Indiana, out from the heart of the America that he later was to stand against for its betrayal of its ideals.

These are a beautiful people, a brave people, not afraid.

There is quiet as we leave this world. The sky is gray. People file [by] us slowly and take the somewhat bitter drink. Many more must drink. Our destiny. It is sad that we could not let our light shine in truth, unclouded by the demons of accident, circumstance, miscalculation; error that was not our intent, beyond our intent.

I hope that someone writes this whole story. It is not "news." It is more. We merge with millions of others, we are subsumed in the archetype.

People hugging each other, embracing, we are hurrying—we do not want to be captured. We want to bear witness *at once.*

We did not want it this way. All was going well as Ryan completed first day here. Then a man tried to attack him, unsuccessfully, at same time, several set out into jungle wanting to overtake Ryan, aide, and others who left with them. They did, and several killed. When we heard this we had no choice. *We would be taken.* We have to go as one, we want to live as Peoples Temple, or end it. We have chosen. It is finished.

Hugging & kissing & tears & silence & joy in a long line

Touches and whispered words as this silent line passes. Determination, purpose. A proud people. Only last night, their voices raised in unison, a voice of *affirmation* and today, a different sort of affirmation, a different dimension of that same victory of the human *spirit.*

A tiny kitten sits next to me. Watching. A dog barks. The birds gather on the telephone wires. Let all the story of this People[s] Temple be told. *Let all the books be opened.* This sight . . . o terrible victory

How bitter that we did not, could not, that Jim Jones was crushed by a world that he didn't make—how great the victory.

If nobody understands, it matters not. I am ready to die now. Darkness settles over Jonestown on its last day on earth.

Mailgram to President Carter

J. Brown

December 5, 1978

Among the papers released by the U.S. Department of State under the Freedom of Information Act was a mother's plea about her children's death certificates. Most families of people who died in Jonestown would never be certain about how their relatives had died.

I, J. Brown, as one of the bereaved mothers, I am requesting that the death certificates of the Jonestown tragedy do not be written off as suicides/mass suicides. I lost 4 children, my son Johnny Moss Brown Jr., his wife Ava Brown, 2 grandchildren Stephanie Brown & Michelle Nicole Brown. My children, as well as the rest were homicides and that is the only thing I will accept on a death certificate. We all must share the blame for this tragedy, and may God have mercy on our souls, for not having the forethought or courage to get those people out of there before what we all knew would eventually happen, and did happen. We sit here and allowed 913 people to be murdered, and now we will try to compromise the dead w/the unfounded theory that it was mass suicide. I will accept my share of the blame, as will all of us. We will not compromise the dead—it was homicide and must be stated on the death certificates as homicide, because I for one will not accept a death certificate w/suicide written on it—only homicide.

One

Editorials and Commentary in the Aftermath of Jonestown

November 21-December 26, 1978

In 1978, the top news story of the year was the death of 918 people in a remote area in the jungle of a small South American country.

For many people the story began with the news that on Saturday, November 18, members of Peoples Temple had opened fire on government officials, journalists, and other members of the church at an airstrip near their agricultural community in Jonestown, Guyana. They had killed a U.S. congressman, three journalists, and a church member. After leaving the dead and wounded on the airstrip, they had returned to Jonestown and joined hundreds of their fellow members who were killing each other and themselves with poison.

As government officials struggled to deal with the immediate logistics of aiding the wounded and dealing with the dead, journalists from around the world overwhelmed Guyanese airports and the capital city of Georgetown. The stories of these deaths of Americans in a foreign land unfolded before the world in daily waves of shocking facts, rumors, and images.

Editorials and commentary in the first month after the deaths in Jonestown chronicled responses of overwhelming alarm, attempts to make sense of the incomprehensible, and the need to place blame. London's *Birmingham Post* pondered human susceptibility to collective madness while other papers sought explanations in everything from U.S. tax exemptions for religious organizations to the diversity of the Guyanese population.

The *Oakland Tribune's* editorial remarked on a death toll of four hundred. In the first week after the news of the deaths, the toll climbed to over nine hundred as government officials discovered more bodies in Jonestown. The *San Francisco Examiner,* which had lost a photojournalist in the deaths at the airstrip, investigated allegations that had been made against Peoples Temple before the tragedy. The San Francisco-based *Sun Reporter,* adamant supporters of Peoples Temple, lamented the tragedy and called for action from black churches.

Later commentaries from George F. Will, Huel Washington, Billy Graham, and Michael Novak focused on blame—lunacy, racism, the devil, and socialism.

At the end of the year, the American Institute of Public Opinion released the results of Gallup Poll interviews conducted in December on the Jonestown tragedy and concluded that it was "the most widely followed event of 1978, with a remarkable 98 percent of Americans saying they had heard or read about it." The report went on to say, "Few events in the entire forty-three-year history of the Gallup Poll have been known to such a high proportion of the U.S. public, except such events as the attack on Pearl Harbor in 1941 and the dropping of the atomic bomb on Hiroshima and Nagasaki in 1945."

The following excerpts from editorials and commentary exemplify the impact of the Jonestown tragedy: direct, deep, and disturbing. It was a huge story that continued to develop and disturb long past 1978.

Birmingham Post
November 21, 1978
Jonestown

It takes a lot now to startle the Western world, which has been made insensitive to shock in the twentieth century by incessant examples of collective madness. But one may suspect that, even in a world of bizarre happenings the bizarre horror story emerging from the settlement of the People's Temple religious cult at Jonestown, Guyana, has been received with almost incredulous surprise. Such is the capacity of the United States to generate strange, unlovely and often fanatical sects which gain a dangerous hold over the minds of their followers that the temptation might be to conclude that the New World in attracting the outcasts and unwanted of the rest of the world must have drawn more than its fair share of the crackpots and the gullible. Any such complacency would be unwarranted as quite a cursory study of history would prove.

The fact is that Man, in spite of his all-too-high opinion of himself, is only too liable to mass reactions to stimuli that lead him into collective madness and wickedness which can be on a vast scale. What causes a Jonestown bout of madness and wickedness to make such a marked impact on dulled world sensibilities is that it is on a small enough scale to be completely comprehensible.

Virginian Pilot
November 21, 1978
Blood on the Land of the Waters

While the shame of what happened was not Guyana's fault, the characteristics of the country contributed to tragedy. Sandwiched between Surinam and Venezuela on South America's northeastern bulge, Guyana, once a British colony, is the only English-speaking country in South America. Its name in a local Indian tongue means "land of waters," and the country is mainly tropical rain forest cut by many rivers. It has a semi-socialist, democratic government. The racial composition of the fewer than 1 million inhabitants is mixed: largely East Indian, with black, creole, American Indian, and European minorities. More than half the people are Christian, a third Hindu, a tenth Moslem.

The diversity of races and beliefs implies a need for tolerance, like that in the United States, that would allow a religious sect, however different, to flourish in so remote a spot. The seed was transplanted there. It bore bitter fruit.

Sacramento Bee
November 21, 1978
Death in Guyana

The purpose of the lives of the members of the People's Temple was always baffling, and now is frightening. Whether the hundreds of deaths at the camp were a horrible admission of failure and remorse over the violence at the airport—or a gruesomely orchestrated fulfillment of Rev. Jones' doomsday prophecies—the intensity of the Temple members' commitment to the sect is terrifying. That blind loyalty may have been a spontaneous outgrowth of their life of austerity and insularity and their mass paranoia when their faith was investigated. Or it may have been beaten into them by a single man gone mad with his power. Either way it is frightening.

New York Post
November 21, 1978
Guyana Horror Story

Ryan and the newsman with him were trying to help young people who had mistakenly seen in Jones an answer to present-day frustrations. A number of other sects offer the same package deal—all they require is complete obedience, a turning away from parents and friends, and money.

The lesson for the young in this tragic affair is that there are no answers in false gods. The lessons for parents and the rest of us is, that it is time for a federal investigation of the many sects now promising so much, but providing so little, and many with large tax exemptions.

Oakland Tribune
November 22, 1978
After Guyana—What Could Happen

The emotionalism over Guyana shouldn't be allowed to prompt witch hunts against anybody who belongs to a cult or commune.

Nobody's calling for investigations of every commune in the country—yet. But the thinking could go this way: Jim Jones once hobnobbed with the country's leading politicians. If he can persuade 400 people to kill themselves, what are some of the other cultists going to do? The authorities had better find out before it's too late.

After all, situations far milder than Guyana led to the inquisitions and witch hunts of the past.

Admittedly, no one is likely to be hung as a witch in the twentieth century.

But it's a fair bet there will be calls for spying on small cults throughout the country in the name of preventing another Guyana. It's easy to visualize someone who's upset by a commune next door demanding an investigation, and whispering, "Remember Guyana."

San Diego Union
November 22, 1978
A Message in Massacre

Because America is proud of its tradition of religious tolerance, our society and its laws give the benefit of the doubt to radical religious cults that test the limits of their constitutional right to exist. Our courts are reluctant, and rightly so, to try to protect people from fanatical cults that seem to rob them, in the name of religion, of their ability to make decisions in their own interest.

Do efforts to spirit such people away amount to rescue—or to kidnapping? Two American lawyers prominent in civil rights actions were on the scene at Jonestown last weekend, retained by Jones to defend the Peoples Temple. Jones was complaining of "religious persecution" as complaints were mounting that what had started as a religious sect had turned into something sinister.

At what point did Jones and the more fanatic of his followers forfeit their claim to the tolerance of a civilized society? When the guns barked at the Kaituma airstrip—or much earlier? Conscience tells us that this nightmare might have been averted if the pleas and the petitions on behalf of some of the captives of Jones's hypnotic preaching had received a more concerned response many months ago.

San Francisco Examiner
November 22, 1978
Jones and the Politicians

Some of them are never going to admit they made a mistake, not even as they view the pictures of those bodies of the poisoned and the shot, stacked as far as the eye can see at Jonestown. A few of these politicians will fashion for themselves a platform of sanctimony high in the ozone of ultraliberalism and maintain until Judgment Day that Jones really was a lovely and "sensitive" fellow when they knew him (and got his political support) . . .

One can understand how Jones, with his captivating personality and skillful articulation and dispensation of aid to unfortunate people could have won over an unsuspecting person—even a high office holder. But after a time, after the early bloom of the Jones movement, there was no reason to be unsuspecting. For the signs were ample that the movement was engaged in the worship of Jones and that all was not right in the ways he exerted his peculiar power . . .

The truth is that he had become liberal chic here and was embraced by people who wanted his support and didn't ask enough questions. We hope this will be a lesson to our leaders not to cater to whatever flaky group comes along, in an effort to capitalize off it politically.

Sun Reporter
November 23, 1978
The Tragedy and the Challenge

In a situation in which, out of the blue, scores—even hundreds—of our loved ones, friends, and neighbors willingly demonstrate their belief in a cause so great that they are prepared to die for it, we who live must wonder at the great chasm of inadequacies in our midst, which prevented us from giving these departed ones a cause so intensely promising that they were prepared to live for it . . .

The churches of the land, and especially the Black churches of San Francisco, might well emulate the commitment of Peoples Temple, which brought so many people together under their banner because they believed this religious institution was totally committed to changing the sordid circumstances of their lives. Peoples Temple members not only felt their united efforts could change their community, but also through suffering and perseverance that they might leave a legacy of hope and inspiration to the oppressed of the world.

The Black churches, which in ages past have served as a refuge in the dark days of the Black experience, must hold high the banner of the Christian faith, proclaiming through action that the gospel of Christ is a vibrant, dynamic, life-giving concept, and especially that Christianity is a commitment that men live for, rather than one that they die for.

George F. Will in the *Washington Post*
November 26, 1978
Wild Religions

The most recent deferment of the upward spiral of history, the carnage in Guyana, has a riveting repulsiveness: What cold flame burns in adults who serve "communion" of Kool-Aid and cyanide to children? The episode reminds: Madness can be a communicable disease.

The Peoples Temple is to a real temple what the Symbionese Liberation Army was to a real army: a lunatic charade. It is another demonstration, in a century replete with them, of how far, physically and morally, people will go to slake the fatal thirst for patent medicine for the soul, medicine promising a feeling of completeness and meaningfulness.

Huel Washington in the *Sun Reporter*
November 30, 1978
Looking Back on Jonestown: The Real Culprit Is America

For a long time the world will ask itself why more than 900 people, adults and children, would find the trials of everyday living so unbearable that they were willing to give up their lives rather than endure them any longer.

No one will ever know the answer, because the principals are all dead. But it doesn't take an expert to see that there are quite a few people who are dissatisfied with the dreams that America offers before dashing its citizens' hopes with deceit, bias, and contradictions.

Short-sighted individuals will blame a deranged preacher named Jim Jones for the murder of a U.S. congressman, three members of the media, a disenchanted follower, and 915 faithful believers. That's too easy.

The real culprit is the institution that America has become. The fundamental principles of liberty, justice, and freedom for all, with emphasis on the rights of others, have been ground under by racism, dishonesty, deceit, and mistrust.

Billy Graham in the *New York Times*
December 5, 1978
On the Devil in Mr. Jones

One may speak of the Jones situation as that of a cult, but it would be a sad mistake to identify it in any way with Christianity.

It is true that he came from a religious background but what he did and how he thought have no relationship to the views and teachings of any legitimate form of historic Christianity . . .

Apparently Mr. Jones was a slave of a diabolical supernatural power from which he refused to be set free.

He was like a drug addict or an alcoholic who refuses to admit his need or seek help from the only one who could have set him free—God!

Michael Novak in the *Washington Star*
December 17, 1978
Jonestown: Socialism at Work

If Jonestown was a religious colony, why did it have no church, no chapel, no place of prayer? It had a day care center, a school, a clinic. The religion of Jonestown was explicitly and unequivocally socialism, not Christianity. The cult in Jonestown was socialism . . .

Those who are attracted to socialism by its moral ideals—by a kind of religious feeling for equality and justice—find it hard to face its actual practical results. Of Jonestown, Mort Sahl said, "Socialists don't do that." The awful truth is that they do. In more places than Jonestown, socialism begins in mysticism and ends in terror. It is the fundamentalism of our time.

PART Two

Beginning in Indiana and
Onward to California

Jim and Marceline Jones and a small group of parishioners established Peoples Temple church in Indianapolis, Indiana, in 1955. The founders based their bylaws for the small, independent Pentecostal church on temperance, a system of tithing, modesty, and total abstinence from narcotics, alcohol, and "every other habit-forming substance." In 1960, the church became affiliated with the Disciples of Christ.

Peoples Temple held a variety of church services several days a week, including evangelism, spiritual healing, and an early evening youth service. Their pastor, Jim Jones, delivered sermons on current events, class conflicts, and socialism to a racially integrated congregation and visitors from other churches. The members ran a popular free restaurant for the city's poor, forced the desegregation of local businesses, and operated nursing homes. Peoples Temple hosted weekly television and radio programs featuring their dynamic preacher and their vibrant integrated choir. The church became well known in the Indianapolis press for the members' integration activities and for their assertions of their pastor's gifts as a healer.

In 1965, Peoples Temple relocated to Mendocino County, in Northern California. Not everyone from Indiana made the move, but more than one hundred members did. While they were building a new church in Redwood Valley, they continued their outreach to new members and held services and meetings in their homes and in borrowed churches. In 1969, they opened their new church with a swimming pool, an animal shelter, gardens, and a community kitchen for their active, three-hundred-member congregation.

Peoples Temple began holding services in San Francisco and Los Angeles in 1970. Two years later, they purchased large churches in both cities and set up counseling sessions after services to help new members with their legal, medical, and financial problems. By 1973, their recruiting drives in African American communities had increased their membership to over twenty-five hundred. Tens of thousands of people, including politicians and members of other congregations, attended Peoples Temple services in California between 1970 and 1977. Some people attended one service. Others attended periodically. Several thousand joined the church and participated regularly in services, meetings, and community outreach activities.

As the membership grew, Peoples Temple expanded its businesses, became active in electoral politics, established communal houses, and purchased a fleet of buses. The members traveled together to services along the West Coast, to events they hosted in cities across the country, and to demonstrations on behalf of the causes they championed, including freedom of the press and civil rights. They continued to offer healings at their services and to attract media attention to their community activities as well as their religious practices.

Letter to Lynetta Jones
Marceline Jones
September 27, 1954

Jim Jones started his ministerial practice in Indianapolis as a student pastor in a Methodist church in 1952. By 1954, he was renting his own small church and offering an eclectic range of preaching styles. On the strength of his compelling performance at healing services, pastors from a larger church, the Laurel Street Tabernacle, invited him to hold services there. In a letter to Lynetta Jones, her mother-in-law of six years, Marceline Jones shared her excitement over the possibility of new opportunities for her husband.

Dearest Mom,

I feel that I must write you of the latest developments in the life of your beloved son. Through all of our tests and hardships I had faith that Jimmy would be something special. This, however, is beyond our fondest dreams.

As I told you in the last letter, we were unable to seat all the people in the other church. Remember Brother Price? He's opened his church to Jimmy. He has even offered him the church in the event of his retirement. We started worshipping there yesterday. Jimmy has a deliverance service on Sunday afternoon at 2:30 p.m. Yesterday, even Rev. Price's church was packed. They had to drag out benches. Saturday night in Cincinnati 200 were turned away. Well over 1000 stayed.

Now, I am anxious to get you in one of these services. If you could only come to be here on Sunday afternoon. I'll be calling you. I send you love and compassion. Hoping to see you soon.

Love, Marceline

from "As a Man Thinketh, So He Is," in the *Herald of Faith*
Jim Jones
May 1956

In 1956, Jim Jones accepted a Certificate of Ordination of Independent Assemblies of God that listed his local church as Peoples Temple "with complete autonomy." On the back of the certificate he wrote:

> Only requirement is that ministers practice the Love of Christ and live honorably and practice every aspect of integrity in his pastoral and business relationships. This was given in honorary recognition without my request for our good work as an independent church in Indianapolis, Ind. I naturally accept their ordination in that it required no endorsement of a limited creed, dogmatic ritual or narrow religious restrictive fellowship.

> Later that year, Jones organized his own evangelical convention, featuring a famous healing evangelist who helped draw thousands of people to the event. The *Herald of Faith*, a journal that served the communities of independent Pentecostal churches and advertised healing conventions in the U.S. and Canada, published Jim Jones's article on Christianity, "As a Man Thinketh, So He Is," on the front cover of their May 1956 issue.

Christianity like a watch needs to be wound if it is to start running. The Word states that "He that hungereth and thirsteth after righteousness shall be filled." We cannot progress with God until we see if there is something to answer our quest for truth. Is there any Divine response to man's yearning for a transformed life? Is progress merely a lifting of oneself "by his own bootstraps?" Is what we hear from Heaven but the echo of our own pleading cry?

In everything from the lowest cell to the highest of God's creations, MAN, there is an urge for a fuller, more abundant life. Everyone reaches anxiously after perfection. The religious urge is found in the life quest. It is the cry for life turned into the cry for a better life. And the moment we say "better" we have standards, and the instant we acquire standards we have religion. As long as people want to live fully and better we will be religious. The forms of religion may come and go but the spirit of religion is deathless from age to age. For it is the cry for life, happiness and peace . . .

We can be destructive or constructive, defeated or successful. We actually create situations by our thoughts and words. We bring life by the words of power affirmed by faith in Jesus Christ or we may bring the power of Hell upon us by negative or destructive ideas. St. James informs us we must first be drawn away by our own lusts (wrong attitudes and actions) before we can be tempted or snared by demoniac influences. Many times imaginary troubles become real by telling them too often . . .

As for me and my house, I am going to partake of Moses' revelation which is expressed in the words, "I AM THAT I AM." I am making every effort to [en]gender positive thoughts and deeds of salvation, deliverance, and peace for all mankind because the Bible assures me "as a man thinketh in his heart so is he." Therefore if I have the above attributes it will no longer be the human limited "I" that liveth but "Christ in me, the hope of Glory."

from "Jim Jones as Seen through the Eyes of Those He Loved"
Marceline Jones
Early 1970s

In the early 1970s, Peoples Temple began documenting the history of their organization by taping interviews with their members. The transcribed accounts were often used for articles in their publications, including their newspaper, *Peoples Forum*, and in press releases and drafts of books they planned to publish.

In her interview, Marceline Jones covered her early relationship with Jim Jones, her feelings about his call to the ministry, and her experiences with racism in Indiana in the 1950s. She recounted how Jones's services had begun to include elements of evangelical and deliverance traditions such as speaking in tongues and the laying on of hands for healings, and how he had begun to use discernment and prophecy to reveal people's inner impulses and to predict future events. She described the challenges Jim Jones had encountered as he insisted on integrated services that finally led them to establish an independent church.

I met Jim when he was a high school senior and worked fulltime as an orderly in the hospital where I was a senior in nurse's training. I first encountered him when I sent for an orderly and he answered my call. A young pregnant woman had died from trichinosis, a disease contracted from eating raw pork. He helped me prepare her body for the undertaker. He was visibly touched by the suffering of her family.

Jim was handsome, brilliant, and ambitious. But the thing I noticed about him first was the sensitivity and concern he exhibited. As the months passed, I became more aware of the attributes I mentioned first. We worked together in the hospital, started dating, and I fell in love. He pursued me diligently. I often teased him by saying, "I married you to get rid of you." But the truth is, I knew there was something special about him. I saw greatness. But little did I know how great he would become. Just as he pursued me once he decided I was the one he wanted, he has pursued truth—once he decided to live and to die to free the oppressed of the world. He didn't have to do it, but he did . . .

It was Jim who first made me aware of the race problem. He was a high school basketball star and quit the team because the coach referred to black players on an opposing team with racial epithets. He left a barbershop with an unfinished haircut because a barber said he wouldn't cut a black man's hair. He was hitchhiking between college and home when a man who picked him up spoke of blacks in a derogatory manner and he demanded to be let out in an isolated area. These are the examples of things that happened during the year and a half we dated . . .

He was a freshman in college when we were married in 1949—during the McCarthy era, a time when this nation bordered on fascism and political witch-hunts were rampant. Jim bravely opposed injustice during that entire time. He, at a very young age, saw the hypocrisy in the practicing religions in the churches of that day. I remember well him standing in a church auditorium in Bloomington, Indiana and telling the people of his displeasure at seeing such an elegant edifice and the minister's Cadillac parked in front of it when poverty was so evident in the community that the congregation served.

We had been married about two years when he decided to become a minister of the gospel. He was eager to awaken the people to the humanity of Jesus and to let them know that what Jesus was they could also be. Jesus was the first born of many brethren. Although Jim knew the Bible from beginning to end, he emphasized the human service ministry of Jesus Christ and said there must be no creed but the helping ministry of Christ and no law but love.

Jim was twenty when he became a minister. After Jim had been ministering for about one year, he went to a church convention in Columbus, Indiana, where a fellow minister prophesied that he would have a deliverance ministry. That night Jim was the speaker and he was introduced as one who had a ministry of healing and discernment. My reaction to the introduction was one of concern for Jim because I didn't know how he could live up to it.

Imagine my amazement when he got up and he called people out by name and by their social security number and by their disease and their illness and marvelous healings took place. My reaction was one of amazement. It was one of feelings of deep concern and one of being aware of the responsibility of such a ministry. But for three days it was as if I walked on air and I could not feel my feet on the ground and it was difficult for me to even speak. I stood in such awe of this marvelous ministry and I stood feeling the burden of this responsibility that had been placed upon the one that I loved more than anyone in the world . . .

He drew crowds and crowds. There were meetings in Cincinnati, where people would come at two o'clock in the afternoon to get a seat at seven-thirty at night and then crawl in the windows. They'd want his shadow to fall on them. They were begging for him to evangelize around the world. He could've taken that Oral Roberts trip but he wouldn't do it. And I would try to encourage it. I'd say, "This would be a great opportunity." But he would say, "No I've got to stay put and live the life in front of the people. It's easy to hop from one place to the next and collect their offerings and not have to set an example."

I remember one time I went to a restaurant with some black friends and the maitre d' said we needed a reservation and I said, "Wait a minute. I've eaten here many times before without a reservation." They finally gave us a table, but they salted our food so badly that it was impossible to eat. Jim had a television show then and he went on the air and fasted publicly until this one restaurant changed its racist policy.

Jim always tried to be in a position of taking the starch out of people. He attracted the working class people because he was so unaffected. Some of the older members had been very starchy, social climbers, and this one-day-a-week religion suited them fine. But I remember a man coming in his work clothes, and he stood up and he said, "I didn't know whether or not to come to church because if I went home to change I'd miss the service and I didn't know if I should come like this." He had on overalls and he was dirty. And Jim said, "That's quite all right, I want you to feel completely comfortable. I want you to know that I have a huge hole in the seat of my pants right now."

And the religious mentality. God, they were Methodists so they baptized people in this little bowl, and well, baptism didn't mean one thing to Jim, but he thought, "If I'm going to have to baptize people, then I'm going to baptize them." So he drug a horse trough into the church. That whole church had to go through that same thing my parents did, only my parents couldn't escape because he was going to be their son-in-law. But the church people could escape and a lot of them fled, he was just too much for them. He tugged this huge horse tank up on the platform, and he immersed them. Probably wanted to drown them.

And I'd been in the Methodist Church, so all day Saturday, I'd get the hymns together and work out a program—hymn number so and so, Doxology, stand, sit, sing, pray—and he'd spend all day Sunday ignoring the whole thing. He wouldn't even look at it. And the first Easter we had service, we had children there and he asked them in service, "Now what do you want to sing?" And they said, "We want to sing 'Here Comes Peter Cottontail, Hopping Down the Bunny Trail.'" So the whole congregation, this very starchy congregation, sang "Here Comes Peter Cottontail." God, they didn't know what to make of him . . .

In Indianapolis, Indiana, there was a large Assembly of God church called Laurel Street Tabernacle. It was there that Jack Beam was on the Board. It was there that Mother Le Tourneau and her family had been members for years. It was there that Eva Pugh had attended for a long, long time. The pastor of that church, Mr. John L. Price, was a very brilliant man, he had met Jim, he knew of his ministry, and he had asked him to come and upon his retirement become the pastor of that church. Jim went and he was holding, every Sunday afternoon, deliverance meetings. This was a large church that was packed out every Sunday afternoon— and I remember one Sunday afternoon, Jim came to me and he said, "I know by discernment that there are black people coming to this church and the ushers are sitting them on the back row." He gave me the name of the two black women that would be there and he said, "I want them to be sat on the platform." Well, as you know, Jim is never wrong. The two black women came, the ushers sat them on the platform, and as a result of that a Board meeting was called. The Board was upset about the black people being on the platform. As a matter of fact, they did not want black people in their church. They did not want to lose Jim's ministry because he was quite a drawing card, after all, not only as far as members were concerned, but financially. So they made an offer in which they said they would help him establish a church in the black neighborhood. And, without hesitation, Jim said, "There will be no church in the black neighborhood—I will not be a pastor of a black church or a white church. Wherever I have a church all people will be welcome." And with that, he walked out. And with him walked Jack Beam and his family, Mother Le Tourneau and her family, her husband and children, and Eva Pugh. We had no money and so Jim borrowed the money to put a down payment on the church in the inner city part of Indianapolis, Indiana, and that was the first Peoples Temple.

In the beginning, he had a hard time making black people believe that he was sincere and he and his workers knocked on the door of every black family in Indianapolis, Indiana. I think they estimated that they knocked on 10,000 doors. And out of that campaign came a few black people and among them was Archie Ijames. It didn't take Jim long to realize that Archie had ability, he had promise, he was also dedicated and he was made associate pastor of the church . . .

I am convinced that if he had been content to be just a healer, there would have been no evangelist in this world that could have compared to him in drawing crowds, but Jim was too much of a man of principle not to also teach people the truth about living the life of *Godliness, the life of love.* And when he started telling these people that wanted to be healed, and these people that were healed, that living a life of God required something of them, that is when the crowds began to fall off. They didn't want to hear that Jesus meant it when he said: You must feed the hungry, and you must take care of the sick, and from each according to his ability and to each according to his need and that God is no respecter of persons, and that we must live together in peace and harmony with racial and economic equality. When he began to tell them, as Jesus told the rich, young ruler, that in order to enter the kingdom, you must sell all and give it to the poor—they were not interested in hearing this.

However, at the same time that the numbers began to drop, people that did stay were people that wanted to go on to perfection. They wanted to be more Godlike. They wanted to live a life of sharing and a life of selflessness. And so where numbers were sacrificed, quality was gained and we began to develop a church family with ties that were much stronger than any blood tie could be, because we began to know what living for truth, what living for justice, what true living was about.

from "With Jim in Indianapolis," in *The Onliest One Alive*
Hyacinth Thrash
Published in 1995, based on interviews from 1983

Hyacinth Thrash and her sister, Zipporah Edwards, joined Peoples Temple in 1957. They were born in Alabama and grew up there until their family moved to Indianapolis in 1919. Raised as Baptists, they continued to attend their neighborhood Baptist church until 1945, when a new pastor asked for more money from his congregation. Hyacinth was fifty-two years old and "Zip" was in her late forties when they first saw Jim Jones and the Peoples Temple choir on a local television station.

Hyacinth Thrash recounted her family's involvement with Peoples Temple in *The Onliest One Alive: Surviving Jonestown, Guyana*, published in 1995.

I hadn't been going to church for about ten years when I saw Jim on TV. Actually, Zip saw him first. She came running in from the other room, shouting, "I've found my church!" She saw the integrated choir on TV and Jim standing so handsome, and wanted to go.

Zip was living with me at the time at 40th and Graceland in the home I bought in the Butler-Tarkington neighborhood. Zip liked what she saw on TV. It was like Jim was just pulling her. Jim was saying God is no respecter of persons, that all minorities were welcome.

As it turned out, my niece Aileen and I went to Jim's church first to check it out . . .

We were impressed with Jim and the church. He invited us back. A month passed. Then one day a flyer appeared on the doorstep. It said Jim and twelve of his members would be on our block Wednesday night, calling. Well, he came, held our hands and had prayer. It was wonderful.

Jim started out real good, doing for folks. We'd buy canned goods and fix up baskets, helping the underprivileged, like Mexicans and blacks, as Jim called us. I guess that's when we started using the word *blacks*. *Negro* wasn't my name. We always used to say *colored folks*. Really, we should have been called Afro-Americans.

The church was still small when Mildred, Zip and I joined in 1957, but it had quite a few black families. Membership was more than one hundred.

Jim integrated Methodist hospital too. He was going to a black doctor, so the hospital assumed he was black and put him in a black ward. It caused such a ruckus they had to change their policy . . .

Jim had a real good church program going in Indianapolis, and Zip and I helped him. Zip was a real good church worker, real faithful. But I always believed in doing my part, too. I wasn't a slacker . . .

I helped with feeding and healing mostly. I worked in the kitchen, preparing meals and giving out baskets. We fed two hundred people at a time on Sundays for dinner at 10th and Delaware—what he called Peoples Temple. Everybody came—street people, alcoholics, transients. Archie Ijames and Rheaviana Beam were real good at procuring foodstuff with the station wagon. They got overripe produce from the Farmers' Market or meat that would spoil if held over the weekend.

from "We All Made the Move"
Stephan Jones
1978

Marceline and Jim Jones were the parents of a large, integrated family that Jim Jones referred to as his "rainbow family." They adopted their first child in 1953. Five years later, they adopted two children who were born in Korea. Just weeks after their daughter Stephanie was killed in a car accident in 1959, Marceline gave birth to their son Stephan Jones. In 1961, they were the first Caucasian family in the state of Indiana to adopt an African American baby.

Throughout their childhoods, the Jones children were joined by other Temple children in their household—some were formally adopted by the Joneses, some were under the legal guardianship of Marceline Jones, and some lived with them under informal arrangements with the children's relatives.

During the early 1960s, the Jones family traveled to Hawaii, Guyana, and Brazil. In 1963, they returned to Indianapolis. By 1965, the family was planning to move again, this time with their church to Northern California.

In this interview recorded by the Peoples Temple in 1978, Stephan Jones described his early relationship with his parents and the differences he found in people's attitudes toward his family in Indiana, Brazil, and later in Redwood Valley, California.

We lived in Indianapolis up until the early sixties. At that time before we left Indianapolis, Dad was a pastor in a church. The way he could see it he was fighting a losing battle, because people were drawing from him but never making any kind of commitments to him, to his ideas. He knew that in Brazil—which is where we went—and other Third World nations there were people starving that would be appreciative of what he had to offer. He knew he could do something for somebody instead of wasting his life on people who were by no means ready to make any kind of commitment. So we left for Brazil when I was about three years old.

I don't remember much, but I know that Dad got right into setting up an orphanage for all the children whose parents had just died off. The only thing that I knew about was that I never had a shortage of playmates and I just thought it was great because I always had somebody to go out and play with. They never looked down on me for having a black brother because they were all darker complected. I just remember the way we lived because Dad never would live high no matter what. We always would live in the poorest sections of town because we didn't want to lose our identification. You didn't feel right. You didn't feel right living higher than anyone else. But he always made sure that we were fed and we always had the little things that he feels children should have.

I remember that people would constantly be coming to the door wanting food, needing something because they were starving just right and left. We had lived what was considered poor in the United States, but when we went down there it just shocked me to see how people were forced to live [in] so many places. It was hard for me to cope with for a long time because I never even imagined that people could be so degraded, malnourished, just so without anything—I mean they had nothing. They had everything they could do to keep themselves alive and their families alive.

In a place like this Dad always had something to do. He was always getting things done for the orphanage or . . . seeing about somebody. He was away from the house quite a bit. Up till that point growing up, I had always identified with my father more than my mother because he had always presented both sides, the strong figure, but at the same time the loving figure. I didn't see how I needed anything else. But with him gone, I kind of had to turn to my mother. I think from her I got a lot of my compassion. I never felt like I had to prove anything to people, at least not at that time. I felt like I could say I loved somebody and I knew I could cry and not feel like a sissy or weird. So I got a good balance . . .

After being in Brazil for a couple of years, it became evident to my dad that there was going to be some sort of right-wing takeover because there was too much unrest in the people. They were getting tired of living conditions and the way they were being oppressed and Dad was sure of what would happen, so we got out of there. Sure enough, eventually a stronger government was put in power.

We went back to Indiana for a short while, at the most, I think it was a year and a half. It was about that time that I started school. I went to kindergarten. Before that time I had never ventured out into the world much . . . The only thing I knew about the world was my family. It was hard for me because ever since I can remember I had a black brother and I had a Korean brother and sister. Until I was well along in life I was not even told that they weren't my natural brothers and sister. I thought they'd come from the same place I had because we'd always been taught that nobody was any different . . . There was no way I could understand that I was acceptable to these people but my brothers and sister weren't. From the start I was incorrigible, but I guess after a while I learned to cope.

I was only in school about half a year, then we moved out to Redwood Valley because the people were starting to call us on the phone and shoot at us. They would mess with our car. They were just starting to harass us. And Dad. Once again we had to run. We had to get out of there because he wanted to protect his family (not just meaning us—there were other people that were loyal to him that he cared about). We all made the move.

I started first grade in Redwood Valley and, if anything, it was worse . . . We lived in Indianapolis in a poor area, in a black area, so I went to school with black children. But there was nobody black in Redwood Valley's school. It was unbelievable. They acted like they had never seen a black person before. They acted like they were inhuman. You'd hear the chants every day. Finally you got immune to it. There was at least one thing that was different about Redwood Valley—I wasn't acceptable either. We were all unacceptable. My brothers and sister were unacceptable because of their color and I was unacceptable because I accepted them.

"History of the Church in California"
Jack Beam
September 27, 1978

Jack Beam and his wife, Rheaviana Beam, were among the founding members of Peoples Temple in 1955. Along with several other members, they left the Laurel Street Tabernacle to start their own church with Jim and Marceline Jones in Indianapolis. In his recollection, Jack describes his trips out west to scout a new location for Peoples Temple. Jim Jones was interested in Northern California because he thought the area would be receptive to an integrated community and safe from nuclear attack, a threat he often prophesied in his sermons.

I came out first, early in 1964, and toured all of Northern California—Eureka, Ukiah, just looking around. At that time I had come from Brazil with just a short stop in Indianapolis for a few days. I had been sent to scout out a place for us. I only went back to Indianapolis to get some of my things but never returned there to live. Jim and some of the rest of them stayed in Brazil for a while longer. And

Archie had spent the whole time in Indianapolis. I lived in Hayward for that time and worked for General Motors. When Jim left Brazil he returned to Indianapolis for several months, then came out to California with Joe Phillips, held a meeting in Los Angeles, and then the three of us went up to Ukiah, looked around and decided that this was it. This was the summer of 1965. Jim then went back to Indianapolis and sent Marceline and the children out. She bought the property with the house where the Church was later built. Three or four months later about 100 persons (including cats and dogs) came out with Jim and settled in the [Redwood] Valley area. It was about ten families.

At first everyone went to work, anything—picking grapes, picking pears, whatever we could get. Work was hard and hard to get. We began by holding services in Jim's garage. We were part of a peace march up to the courthouse steps in 1968, and there was quite a verbal confrontation. We started the Redwood Valley Church in 1967 and completed it in 1968.

For the longest time Jim held two teaching jobs. There was a day teaching job in the high school at Booneville, and a night civics class at Ukiah High School. He finally gave it up because the driving got to be too much. He used the classes, especially the night class, to interest people in the work. Several of the day students . . . used to travel with Jim daily to school at Booneville. The meetings in the garage were political education and self-analysis, some healing.

This went on for the longest time, perhaps a year and a half till the first expansion to San Francisco. This was done by a joint meeting with Rev. Bedford at a Baptist church, followed by an invite for their congregation to meet at Ukiah, which they did at the fairgrounds. Their congregation came up once more to the opening of the Redwood Valley Church. Jim did some healing. Shortly after, a few meetings were held at Verdella Duncan's (Jim had converted a few of Bedford's people), another place, then at Benjamin Franklin [Middle School]. It spread like wildfire once about six families were convinced. Soon Benjamin Franklin was full, and a schedule was established where meetings were held on alternate weekends in San Francisco and [Redwood] Valley. About this time, transportation became an issue and they started buying buses. The first we got in late '69 or '70 and by spring 1972 the whole fleet of 11 buses was bought.

from "Following Jim to California," in *The Onliest One Alive*
Hyacinth Thrash
Published in 1995, based on interviews from 1983

Hyacinth Thrash and her sister, Zipporah Edwards, left their home in Indianapolis in 1967 to join their friends and church in Redwood Valley, California. Before she moved to California, Hyacinth was partially paralyzed from an operation on her spine. Once in California, the sisters bought a home, cared for several disabled residents, and attended Peoples Temple services in Redwood Valley and San Francisco. They moved to the church's communal apartments in San Francisco in 1976. By this time many members referred to Jim Jones as Father. Some called him Dad. Others, like Hyacinth, always called him Jim.

Jim picked Redwood Valley in Northern California 'cause it was supposed to be safe from nuclear attack. He said he had a secret cave off Highway 101, but I never seen it. The men in the church said it was big enough to store food and supplies and hold all our members we had in Redwood Valley at that time. But after Jim started churches in San Francisco and Los Angeles, he quit talking about nuclear holocaust . . .

Ukiah was in grape growing country. At that time Ukiah was more southern in its attitude toward blacks. Before our church moved there, there was only one black family in the whole town. Zip and I were the only blacks in our apartment building . . .

The reason Zip and I moved from Ukiah to Redwood Valley, a suburb of Ukiah, was to buy a care home from retirees who'd been taking mental patients from Mendocino State Hospital. This was when Governor Reagan started closing down big hospitals and putting patients out in the community if they were well enough to live on the outside.

We bought a lovely four-bedroom ranch house on one and a quarter acres of land and took in four lovely ladies as "care" patients. I was just crazy 'bout our home . . . We loved it in the Valley. We had our own grape arbor by the house. And pears! Zip and I put up 150 quarts of pear stuff—pear preserves, pear butter, pear sauce . . . And we canned peaches, pretty as a picture. We even made zucchini pickles. And they were good! I never even knew you could make pickles from zucchini till we moved to California. And corn! We canned corn and froze corn. Got so we never even cold-packed string beans anymore. We just froze them in large plastic bags. They tasted just like fresh beans. We had tomatoes too, and made our own chili sauce. . . .

I was so sad to leave our patients when we moved to San Francisco . . . We lived on Geary Street, in a nice apartment near the Peoples Temple. Buses picked us up to go to church on Sundays. In the service it was my job to sit with visitors and tell them what a nice place the church was, the wonderful things it did.

We were supported by Jim. The church paid the rent. We bought our own groceries with money Jim gave us. The only dinner we ate at the church was Sunday dinner. He said we were to get a hundred dollars out of our Social Security checks, but we never did. Our apartment had two bedrooms. Zip and I took in two blind people, the Mercers, a couple who joined after a revival in Pittsburgh. Jim sent for them. Jim knew we'd take good care of them, and we did. "You're better to us than our own people," they said.

from "No Haloes Please"
Patricia Cartmell
1970

In Redwood Valley, Peoples Temple started holding Tuesday evening services called "Deeper Life Catharsis meetings for the development of our Spiritual Growth." Patricia Cartmell, who had come with Peoples Temple from Indiana, chronicled her experience at one of these meetings in 1970.

There appeared to Jim in revelation an airplane, with lights flashing on and off, and the pilot in great consternation with sweat on his brow. We meditated for the pilot that he would feel the restraining power of love and be kept from dropping his load of bombs and bringing devastation to many innocent people.

A period of catharsis followed, a very painful experience but oh so necessary, in which each member of the body was encouraged to stand and get off his chest everything that was in any way a hindrance to fellowship between himself and another member or between himself and the group, or the leader even, Jim in his utter honesty not desiring nor seeking immunity from the exposure of his own faults. And Jim was faithful to lead off with the confession [of] faults, not asking us to do anything which he is either unwilling to do or unable to do.

Jim Pugh then spoke up concerning a number of things which were troubling him, and from there different ones arose to make known their hidden frustrations, doubts and hurts. The catharsis was greatly needed, it opened the clogged channels for the flow of love, which in response to our limited obedience swept in and met many needs of the people. We are reminded that catharsis is not a new approach to the solution of human problems, there being an old but seldom obeyed biblical injunction, "Confess your faults one to another and pray one for another that ye might be healed."

The remaining highlight of the service was our beloved leader's reaction to a picture in the newspaper of a young mother who drowned her baby because she had no food for it. So touched he was by this tragic act that he wept much over it. He wept for the poor pitiful starving masses everywhere, and particularly for those unfortunate Viet Namese who were being oppressed by our ruthless war machine. He is greatly appalled by the merciless napalm bombing of whole villages on the slim chance that Viet Cong are hiding therein. (Napalm is a substance like jellied gasoline which sets fire to everything it comes in contact with, and the utter horror of it is that human beings are not immune to it and are all too often victimized by it. Mothers and babies along with everyone else!)

Returning home after the service I felt so clean, and I pledged myself that I should always be open to introspection and catharsis, the acknowledgement and confession of my faults.

"Chimp in the Valley"
Temple Reporter
1973

Pictured here is Mr. Muggs, our local chimpanzee-in-residence, together with his adopted mom, Joyce Touchette. Grossly mistreated, Muggs was rescued by Rev. Jim Jones and patiently nursed back to health.

Only 18 months old, he has the intelligence of a four year old child. He will be full grown at five years, will weigh 200 lbs., and have the strength of ten men. Muggs loves children and animals, but is wary of adults, especially strangers. His reasons deserve our sympathy. For every baby chimp that is brought to the U.S., one mother chimp is killed. Out of seven thousand chimps exported to the United States, only seven hundred survive the taxing journey. Quite naturally, Muggs distrusts strangers, and is always alert when they are around. It may sound anthropomorphic, but Muggs will follow every command of Pastor Jones, and will

CHIMP IN THE VALLEY

MR. MUGGS AND HIS ADOPTED MOM, JOYCE TOUCHETTE

Pictured above is Mr. Muggs, our local chimpanzee-in-residence, together with his adopted mom, Joyce Touchette. Grossly mistreated, Muggs was rescued by Rev. Jim Jones and patiently nursed back to health.

Only 18 months old, he has the intelligence of a four year old child. He will be full grown at five years, will weigh 200 lbs., and have the strength of ten men. Muggs loves children and animals, but is wary of adults, especially strangers. His reasons deserve our sympathy. For every baby chimp that is brought to the U.S., one mother chimp is killed. Out of seven thousand chimps exported to the United States, only seven hundred survive the taxing journey. Quite naturally, Muggs distrusts strangers, and is always alert when they are around. It may sound anthropomorphic, but Muggs will follow every command of Pastor Jones, and will defend him even when anyone comes up casually to pet the chimpanzee. Muggs likes to be in church services, and will keep rhythm to the music by tapping his feet. A modern, spacious habitat is presently being built near the animal shelter at the Temple, to house Muggs when he grows a little older.

Mrs. Touchette was one of the many who offered to keep and care for Mr. Muggs, and his antics have made him the delight of her family. Muggs is a gourmet. On his list of favorite foods: salad with garlic dressing, lasagna, whipped cream, "Mounds" candy bars, nuts, bolts, screws, and rocks. A somewhat particular eater, Muggs prefers rocks found on the roof of the Touchette house to those lying on the ground. When asked his opinion of life at the Touchette's, Mr. Muggs grinned and replied: "**Wahoo!**"

The "Chimp in the Valley" article, clipped from the Peoples Temple publication the *Temple Reporter*.

defend him even when anyone comes up casually to pet the chimpanzee. Muggs likes to be in church services, and will keep rhythm to the music by tapping his feet. A modern, spacious habitat is presently being built near the animal shelter at the Temple, to house Muggs when he grows a little older.

Mrs. Touchette was one of the many who offered to keep and care for Mr. Muggs, and his antics have made him the delight of her family. Muggs is a gourmet. On his list of favorite foods: salad with garlic dressing, lasagna, whipped cream, "Mounds" candy bars, nuts, bolts, screws, and rocks. A somewhat particular eater, Muggs prefers rocks found on the roof of the Touchette house to those lying on the ground. When asked his opinion of life at the Touchettes', Mr. Muggs grinned and replied: "Wahoo!"

"Guide for the Hostess"
Early to mid-1970s

Peoples Temple members were constantly on the move to services up and down the state of California. Every other weekend, they traveled from their Redwood Valley church to the San Francisco church for a Friday night service, and then drove through the night, picking up more members as they went, for services in Los Angeles. They made the return trip in time to go to work and school on Monday mornings. By 1974, their caravans were eleven buses long. They also traveled together on trips across the country and to Mexico.

The members maintained the buses in specially built Peoples Temple garages. They developed very detailed written procedures for keeping the drivers awake for these long drives and for keeping restless passengers calm and healthy. Many members believed that Jim Jones had the ability to protect them from traffic accidents if they meditated together at regular intervals. Members also bought anointed cloths, oils, and photos of Jim Jones to protect them from misfortune and illness.

GUIDE FOR THE HOSTESS

The following information is designed not as an absolute format you are to follow, but rather—as a guide, along with your common sense as to what is needed as circumstances change. For the most part, you will find it will prove out—but in the extenuating circumstances that come along the road you will have to improvise as needed, and make-do with what you have. The one invaluable suggestion would be CONSULT with others . . . in emergencies. Take the extra moment to consult if it is at all possible.

SANITATION

Aside from seeing that your passengers have no elimination or bowel problems—this is probably your one major objective.

ALCOHOL should be used each time before handling the food; if you have to scratch your face or head—clean your hands again. Whether or not there are germs, it will make the food more appetizing to your passengers if you take the sanitation measures. . . .

Do not try to save the styrofoam cups. In the heat of summer, the milk sours quickly in it—and you cannot get them clean at the road stops.

If you have enough (and it should be) plastic silverware for the trip, please do not try to save it. THE MENU & UTENSILS should be thought of together so that you have what is needed to serve. The following sheets have also listed the supplies you will need. IF YOU MAKE CHANGES OR SUBSTITUTES, MAKE THE CHANGES ALL THE WAY ACROSS THE PAGE . . . SO THAT SERVING IS KEPT IN MIND, WITH THE CHANGE. . . .

PLASTIC BAGS FOR TRASH SHOULD BE PASSED IMMEDIATELY AFTER PEOPLE HAVE EATEN, AND GET IT OFF OF THE BUS AT THE NEXT STOP.

BATHROOM FACILITIES

A mop and broom should be carried along with you. When you stop along the way . . . BE SURE you take roll before and after. Do not leave this to the "person setting next" to be responsible. YOU AS HOSTESS ARE RESPONSIBLE TO OUR FRIEND . . . no one else. Tell the driver you will check the facilities, and be *sure* that both men & women restrooms are clean. If we mess them up, quickly sweep and damp mop them—It is important to caution our people not to TELL folks that we are Peoples Temple, but someone will slip and say it . . . so we must leave a clean trail. Whenever possible, our people should CLEAN up the places as they go—picking up trash as our friend always has us do. PLUS, THE EXERCISE IF NECESSARY for your passengers who have been sitting so long.

JOGGING

Exercise your passengers every two hours during the day, and every four hours at night . . . Have them stand and move about . . .

MOUNTAINS
Caution!

GOING OVER MOUNTAINS . . . on a long rise or descent where the ***EARDRUMS*** are affected, be sure that you waken your people and try to have them awake. They might sing, etc . . . (*just on going **up** & coming **down** mountains*)

NURSING

If you do not have a nurse on board to do it . . . be sure that you have gotten instructions before leaving from the nurse on the precautions you must take with older people, what to do about laxatives if needed ... etc.

THE PEA BUCKET should have a cover and be dumped and disinfectant kept in it at every stop ... It might be advisable to also use a large plastic bag in it for easier cleaning, especially since some will HAVE to use it for bowel movements—IT "WILL" HAPPEN ... it always does!

UTENSILS

Your utensils that will be needed are listed with the menu ... The sharp KNIVES must be watched carefully ... Keep these at the back of your closed rack ... KNOW where you have placed anything sharp AT ALL TIMES ...

REST

Keep it quiet at night ... SEE THAT HOSTESS AND DRIVERS GET THEIR REST ... If the bus gets too raucous or noisy, do not shout angrily at our people if you can help it ... rather ... get them laughing, and perhaps sing ... TOO OFTEN, WE HAVE SEEN THAT THE MECHANICAL FAILURES COINCIDE WITH NASTY TEMPERAMENT ... OF DRIVERS, HOSTESSES OR PASSENGERS ... When we had the happy youth on a bus with a damaged oil apparatus ... and they sang—the bus rolled on in spite of mechanical failures .... Before that it had broken down time, after time, after time ... Father put the youth on it and they began singing. ... and that bus was fine from then on in ... His energy is always there. We call on it through our positive and joyous spirits, which we all know of course.

REMIND

remind passengers regularly of what is expected of them ...

TREATS & FUN

Plan a few treats and some fun ... singing, or testimonies along the way. Testimonies give folks a chance to express themselves, and it turns their minds to our friend ...

A little candy, a little ice—extra, or in their drink, BEWARE OF GUM

AT NIGHT AS IT MIGHT BE SWALLOWED. . . . cookie or pastry if you can get it reasonable . . . or watermelon . . .

TRY TO KEEP THE SPIRITS LIGHT and happy and focused on our friend. This should not be hard to do in view of where we are going !!!!!!!!!!!!!!!!!!!!

DRIVERS

They have a lot of information usually, most of them have been on the road a lot—and will know procedures if you are not certain. Above all, be courteous to them so that the passengers will be confident in them . . . BE VERY VERY ATTENTIVE TO THEIR NEEDS WHEN THEY ARE DRIVING, AND ESPECIALLY WHEN YOU HAVE THE NIGHT SHIFTS. . . . OR WHEN YOU ARE AWARE THE DRIVER IS GETTING WEARY . . .

A cool cloth on the back of his neck or her neck will often waken them . . . If you need to, and with their permission—an iced cloth they can wipe their face and forehead with . . . or ICE TO MUNCH ON . . . *Get—your—own sleep,* **too!**

TALKING WITH DRIVERS

Your constant chatter can actually become monotonous to them and put them to sleep. Ask questions and generally carry on a conversation, but do not DO *all of* the talking . . . mostly, let *them* do the talking. It is harder for them to fall asleep if they are telling you some interesting experience they had in the church, or before they came . . .

DRIVER SNACKS. . . .

These are designed to help keep the drivers awake . . . so do pay attention to their preferences . . .

Note they fall into group-categories:

#1 basically salty items with a little more substance to them—chewy . . . USU-ALLY 2 of this group. . . .

#2 . . . and #3 are sweets . . . Some drivers like the hard candies to stay awake . . . See that there are always "some" sweets in the snack pack. If they get a sudden drop in energy, the sugar will give a quick pickup, but about 20 minutes later there will be a drop in blood sugar and they will tire . . . the sweets should be eaten at latter part of the shift, and steadily thereafter or they will react sleepily . . . VITAMIN E AND C . . . should be in their packet, as it is helpful . . . . several Vita C and E (at least an hour apart) will keep them more alert . . . Of course we all know not to take the two kinds together as our friend has told us they cancel out each other when taken together.

#4 Fresh fruit has a different kind of sugar, and they will not get the drop in blood sugar afterwards . . . they stay "up" for about an hour after eating fruit and the drop in blood sugar is very slow . . . Oranges are perhaps best to keep them alert . . .

#5 is primarily for entertainment . . . the road is boring and the pickles and sour items usually wake them up . . . not all drivers like them . . . ask . . .

#6 If they drink their two sodas for the shift, and still want something cold to drink—see that they have Tang or instant iced tea, and mix with ice and water for them . . . the cold drinks are invaluable to keep them alert and awake . . . the hostess can drink all she wants of these, also . . . on the return trip, she can have sodas . . . if she has them on the trip going—she will find that the passengers want them too and will not be very understanding when they cannot have them!

#7—2 sodas of their choice, and all the ice they need should be available to the drivers for every shift.

ICE CAN BE GOTTEN AT THE DRIVERS STOPS, WHERE YOU CAN TRY TO GET CRUSHED ICE FOR THE DRINKS . . . IF YOU CANNOT, THEN GET THE CUBES . . . BUT SEE THAT YOU HAVE "SOME" ICE FOR THE PASSENGER DRINKS AND ICE FOR YOUR DRIVERS . . . DAY AS WELL AS NIGHT . . . SOME DRIVERS CAN "CHEW" ICE AND STAY AWAKE BETTER THAN EATING AT NIGHT . . . It also keeps temperamen[ts] sweeter, which keeps down *repair* costs on the buses. . . . ice is cheap compared to DOWN time on the road which costs extra *food* as well as money and time . . . and may make people miss a plane. . . . Important to keep the spirits high, so think in terms of surprises and pleasing the folks . . . as much as we possibly can, and keeping all cool and comfortable as possible.

PART Three

Seekers, Believers, and Gatherers

Each individual who joined Peoples Temple had a unique relationship to the church and to Jim Jones. Some people joined because of the integrated and lively church services. Peoples Temple offered ways to be involved right away—a place to roll up your sleeves and get to work with friendly people. There were potlucks after church and community activities focused on children, seniors, and pets. Many people who joined believed in Jones's healings, which were often staged with the help of long-term, trusted members of the church. Still other newcomers believed in Jones's psychic abilities or, like Jones, believed in reincarnation. Some joined because Peoples Temple helped them to deal with financial and legal problems. Several people who joined were social workers who had seen members of People Temple helping their clients. Others joined because of the political messages that Jim Jones included in his sermons—political messages he supported with arguments that seemed logical and were filled with calls to action. He often referred to Rev. Martin Luther King Jr., President John F. Kennedy, Robert F. Kennedy, Malcolm X, the Vietnam War, Watergate, and apartheid and other international issues, especially those based on racial and economic discrimination, to illustrate the failings of government policies and leadership.

Jim Jones's style of preaching attracted many of the people who joined Peoples Temple. Rev. J. Alfred Smith, who knew Jim Jones and attended some of his services, described his preaching style in "Breaking the Silence: Reflections of a Black Pastor." He noted that his preaching style was consistent with the rhythm and the cadence of black ministers, but that Jones had more authority as a leader of his congregation than a black minister would because he was white. He went on to say:

> The combination drew black people to the church, and it kept them in the church. They not only had a man who could speak their language, they also had

a white leader who could speak the language of the dominant society. And they knew it. They knew they could move forward with that church more than they could with any other. They suddenly had the strength, power, and influence of being white… Jim Jones understood this dynamic and knew that even as his leadership gave his black congregants power, their presence—their sheer numbers—gave him power.

Jim Jones connected directly to people's fears, confusion, grief, and anger. He challenged people to actively question established religious practices and to develop a personal belief system that encompassed ways to create change in their everyday lives and express their commitment to social justice. He offered those who attended Peoples Temple services a community of people from all walks of life and all ages, all striving to make a difference.

"Who Are the Real Radicals?"
Jim Jones
October 1970

Peoples Temple often published Jim Jones's sermons in their newsletters along with service and meeting schedules, prophetic warnings, updates on civil liberties, and advertisements for church businesses. In this sermon published in October 1970, Jones refers to actions and policies of the United States government against Native Americans, African Americans, and the Vietnamese— topics that were well known to his audience. Most of Jones's examples supported his assertions about American society strikingly well, gaining support for his ideas about how to effect change.

There is nothing on earth that contributes more to the mass confusion that we now have about what a true radical is than the news media, the bombers, and the various so called "silent majority" of Americans who call such acts and deeds of violence "radical." Nothing is less genuinely radical in America than violence because we have been saturated with violence from the beginning of our history. Our murdering violence began with efforts to dispossess and kill the American Natives (Indians), which we did in countless military endeavors; for example, the Battle of Wounded Knee at which time our army murdered all of the Indians, men, women and children, while they were on their way to a peaceful religious observation of their ancient and beautiful creed. Again on another occasion under orders of the U.S. Government, blankets were taken from U.S. soldiers who had died of smallpox and were given to American Indians knowing full well that it was an act of genocide (murder) which would enable the U.S. Government to get the land and eliminate the Indians at the same time… Our settlement of the West was a parade of lawlessness and vigilante mobocracy. Yes, violence is as common to our history as cherry pie…

We have to speak with tongue in cheek when we refer to violence as being a radical act in American society when we consider the numerous assassinations of present-day political figures. President Kennedy, according to an intensive study in an article by a nationally famed electronics magazine, was killed by a conspiracy, which involved almost every level of governmental life. Let's look at the violence recently by the hardhat white construction workers who attacked young people merely because they carried out their constitutional right of dissent. Yes, violence is quite characteristic of American life. We use napalm and other anti-civilian weapons on the countless disadvantaged millions in Viet Nam. Surely we have not forgotten the atrocities of My Lai and the pictures in one of the national magazines where our soldiers were shown murdering innocent women and children in the name of protecting them from Communism.

My friend, the genuine radical is not one who acts on the premise that violence is something revolutionary in the American picture. No, the real radical is one who is engaged in a determined struggle to break out of the vicious cycle of violence that is a part of our everyday life… Let us note that this so-called revolutionary violence has not helped the students, the socially deprived Blacks, Whites or Browns in our country, and on the contrary if it has aided anyone, it has been the tyrannical hold of the rich and the super rich in their attempt to suppress all dissent to their right to absolute power. The violence has accomplished nothing but to bring one repressive law after another out of the halls of Congress and State Assemblies. Thus, it well could be that these terrorists are the paid representatives of the wealth establishment of our country, but again is this not the pattern of history?

But the true radical in our Mother Land differs from the assassins, the bombers and the rioters in every respect. The American radicals are not those that seek violence by short circuits to democratic educational policies even though they may call themselves in some instances the New Left. This use of violence attributed supposedly to the liberal Left actually destroyed the possibility for the Left to become a mass movement or effectually bring about any real social change.

Nihilism (senselessness) and hedonism (pleasure seeking) have only succeeded in fragmenting all progressive movements in our country. Certainly we who affirm apostolic equalitarianism and social and racial justice have nothing whatsoever to gain from this insanity of violence, but could it enhance further the stranglehold of the military-industrial complex on the United States which even President Eisenhower warned us in the early 1960s was a danger to our great country?

A Christian must be a radical, for scripture has declared, "I would that thou wert cold or hot because the lukewarm I will spew out of my mouth" (Revelations 3). But, a Christian radical attempts to transform society not by hate, animosity and fear which is now at the very heart of our institutions and souls, but by a positive activism, protest and dissent and non-violent participation in the electoral process. We can bring about total racial and economic justice, and an end to war and poverty in no other manner! Read the requirements for entrance into the Kingdom of God as stated by Jesus of Nazareth in Matthew 25 and consider in concluding this reading the admonition of the Apostle Paul when he said, "Therefore if thine enemy hungers feed him" (Romans 12:20). This is true radicalism of a non-violent, but very constructive nature, which has never once been tried on the America scene!

Personal Histories
1978

Peoples Temple created organizational files that included personal records of many of their members. Lawyers and social workers who belonged to the church often helped other members in dealing with their taxes, traffic accidents, custody issues, name changes, and problems with Social Security and other government benefits. These records also included accounts by and about the members. Many of these were about Jim Jones. Stories about healings and prophecies were often used in Peoples Temple publications and in their solicitations for donations by mail. Some accounts were put in the form of affidavits that they anticipated using in response to lawsuits and to allegations in the press.

In 1978, the Peoples Temple started collecting more detailed biographies. In these documents, known as "Personal Histories," members—teenagers to centenarians—told stories about their ancestry, about their religious backgrounds, about the struggles they had faced in their personal lives, and about the challenges and rewards they had experienced as members of Peoples Temple.

Janice Wilsey recounted the experiences of her Native American family on reservations in California. One element of her story that had a huge impact on her family and many others was the harsh educational system the U.S. government created for Indian children from the 1870s to the 1930s. In the 1970s, when this personal history was recorded and transcribed, few Americans knew that many Native American children had been forced to attend boarding schools far away from their homes and families. Janice Wilsey met Jim Jones when he was teaching adult education classes in Ukiah, California. She joined Peoples Temple in 1967 with her friend Christine Lucientes.

On September 23, 1949, I was born in a very small town in Northern California. I spent the first seven years of my life on an Indian reservation called Round Valley in Mendocino County, California. My people had been relocated to this area at the time of the California Gold Rush. They were herded like cattle by the soldiers. Two thousand survivors of several tribes were put into this stockade in remote Round Valley.

My grandmother told me stories of how her mother, as a little girl, made the long walk. She said that the nights were cold and the mountains were high. The older people who could not make it or just needed to sit for a minute or two along the path were shot and left to die. This was only the beginning of much suffering. Another story told to me by my grandmother was how a young girl from the Wylackie tribe watched as her father, brother, and all the men of the tribe were lined up and shot all at once. The people built a fire with the trees and bush that these men had been cutting for days, not knowing that it was their own funeral pyre they were fixing. She said the fire was big and the smell of the burning bodies made your hair rise on the back of your neck and the smell made you sick to your stomach.

It did not take the white man long before he moved into this valley and formed a town called Covelo. Along with the town he built five bar rooms to sell the alcohol that he brought with him. I will always remember the five bar rooms and two stores that made up this town. What a place to grow up!

Both my mother and father were born and grew up on the reservation and like every child they were taken away—I call it kidnapped—from their parents and sent away to an Indian boarding school. They could not speak their own language and they only saw their parents on holidays and [in] the summertime. Now, this is very hard on a young child. In fact, there are many cases of children who ran away time after time, sometimes traveling many miles over many states only to be returned once again to the boarding school. A lot of times there were as many as five–six suicides during a school term. This was the life of an Indian confined to a plot of land with nothing to look forward to. Even at the boarding school there were guards to keep you within the school.

I will always remember the look on my mom's face when I said I wanted to spend a couple of summer months at an Indian boarding school called Sherman Institute in Southern California. She made it clear that she did not want me to go, because the thought of it only brought her pain. In the early fifties, a law was passed that California Indian children did not have to go away to boarding school, but would go to the public school system. To this day, Indian children in many states are forcefully taken away from their parents and sent to these [boarding] schools. My mom let me go after my dad spoke up and said I should be able to go if that was what I wanted.

Sherman Institute was named after General Sherman, who went through Southern California killing off any Indian tribe that got in his way. What an insult to name the school after such a man. This to me only added more salt to the wound. The two months that I spent at this school I will never forget. We were all given a talk as to what time we are to be in the dorm, for bed checks were at nine o'clock. It had been some time since my bedtime had been that early! I hated the rules and you can bet I broke many of them while there those two months.

It was sad. In fact I cried many times when I thought of the other Indian children, all my age, who never had a water fight or even thought of staying up after the lights were to be out, running up and down the halls—yelling and screaming. To me it was what any young person would do to have fun. But I soon found out that these young people my own race and age were so much oppressed that they did not know how to express themselves. I was withdrawn to a great extent, but to find other Indian children who were far more withdrawn than I was heartbreaking.

I went home from this summer a little more aware of the world around me. I also had another burden of guilt that I did not want to deal with. My dad was put in a Vet hospital because the alcohol he had been drinking for years was beginning to have its effect. One morning he woke up to discover that he could not get out of bed. He was paralyzed in his lower part of his body and he had no use of his hands. I don't think I can ever tell the pain I had to endure watching my dad, who once was a very proud man, deteriorate day by day.

It was not long after my dad became paralyzed that both my brothers started to drink heavily at a very young age. They both came to the conclusion that there was nothing in this world that they wanted and no one that gave a damn about them. By the time I was sixteen, my mom had tried suicide because she could not cope with the pressure of trying to keep our family together. She had been the sole supporter of the family ever since we moved off the reservation, because my dad could not get a job or keep the job—which was no fault of his own. I remember one time he said to me how proud he was of me that I could stand up in front of people and speak my mind. He always had to have a drink before he could walk into a place and ask for a job.

By the time I was fourteen years old, I was using drugs to escape from the unreality of life. I was told by a high school teacher that I might as well take a typing class and office machine class because I would never achieve in college. I had a limit placed on my life. I was told to *forget it* and *don't try*. Well, for the next four years I did cop out by escaping into the world of hard line drugs. Within these years I had tried suicide more than once. I felt that no one cared and if there was hope, I would never find it.

One day I heard of Jim Jones. Christine Lucientes, a friend of mine, said he was different than any teacher she had ever had and she wanted me to come with her to a night class. I went, but before I went I indulged myself with some opium, which had become a daily thing with me, sometimes four–five times a day. At seventeen years of age it helped me to forget the hurt and pain of life. I will never forget that scene as I walked into the classroom that night. An Indian lady that I had known all my life was up in front of the class leading the discussion about the life of the Indian people. She felt at ease enough to get up in front of this group of people and express herself. I could not believe it and I must have stood there looking shocked for some time. Jim Jones looked my way and showed more concern for me than I could ever remember anyone showing. He said he was glad to see me and he found a seat for me to sit up front. This may seem like a small gesture to most, but to me it was not. I would remember this and other things, like the fact that he made sure my friend Christine and I had a ride home after the class at night, when I was at my lowest moments a year later.

I was 18 years old and alone in the city of San Francisco, a very lonely and depressed person. It was the last part of December and a very cold day in my apartment on the fifth floor. That day I reached a very low point. There seemed to be nothing in the way of drugs to bring me out of it. I had taken four tabs of acid and I had no relief, so then I tried some speed, which only depressed me more and I felt the only way to solve the problem was to jump out of the window. Just as I was ready to jump, I remembered the concern that had been shown to me by Jim Jones and I stopped, made a phone call to my parents, who came right down to the city to pick me up. A week later I joined Peoples Temple.

I was at the point that I could not speak one complete sentence without forgetting what I was talking about right in the middle of what I was saying. The drugs most definitely had their effect on my brain. I was one of the first to go through the drug rehabilitation program. What a job the people had on their hands as they stayed by my side around the clock. They tried to get me to talk but I would not do it. In fact, Christine, for the first few months after I had joined Peoples Temple, did the talking for both herself and me. Jim said that he knew I would not talk but I could sing, so the first song I sang was *My Country Tis of Thy People You're Dying* in front of the whole group. It was the first time I had sung before thousands of people. At first I could never make it through without crying, then as time went on I was able to sing the song of my people the whole way through. Time was taken with me to guide me along. It was no easy process to bring me out of the shell that I had around me.

Next came the fully paid college education. I had never given a thought to even try to go to college, for I had been told years earlier to "forget it," in so many words. Jim encouraged me to go to college. He said I had a good mind and I could achieve. I went, although I really didn't believe I could do it. I had been in school a few days when I decided this was not what I wanted, but Jim stepped in again and wrote letters to all my professors asking them to give me all the assistance that they could. He also told them about my life—with this I got the extra attention that I needed. I came out with a straight B average that term.

■ *Christine Renee Lucientes* was a student in Jim Jones's night classes in Ukiah, California, for several months before she joined Peoples Temple in 1967. In this personal history she described her experiences of growing up in the sixties, her family's drug use, her parents' disintegrating marriage, and small-town bigotry.

I grew up pretty much in a middle class atmosphere without the pain of physical deprivation. I, like so many millions more, grew up with the pain of shallow relationships and superficial exchanges. My dad, Jose, bought a tile company in

Ukiah, California, and we moved, my mother, father, brother and sister, and I, from Sacramento to Redwood Valley.

My dad always seemed to be a bitter and restless man and I suppose it was this in his nature that made him seek something outside the routine of his established life and into the budding drug cult of the sixties. Whatever the reasons, his searching wrought dramatic changes to his already shaky family…His quick "Latin" temperament brought much grief to his offspring—yet this one has since come to the realization that he is merely a product of the pain and hurt that society heaped upon him. It was sad that he has always been ashamed of a Latino heritage and denied it with great vehemence. Certainly he was never conditioned to have pride and it never grew under a barrage of vicious teasing, "wetback" etc., that he received as a child.

My mother, Gail, a passive person in many ways yet deeply affectionate, was a buffer to the violence of my dad and I feel indebted to her for what shreds of sanity I managed to salvage. Certainly she suffered as much or more than anyone in the Lucientes's circle.

As my parents experimented with drugs, so did they with people. Our home was always filled with people since I was a small child, but the diversity of our company increased with their psychic ventures into the unknown world of the great stranger—the mind. Drugs were viewed as the mystic vehicle to self-realization and actualization—yet dramatic illuminations and brilliant insights happened while personalities crumbled and deteriorated.

I was given marijuana at the age of fourteen. Already a troubled personality, my problems were magnified and if I got any deep insights, they were lost or absorbed in the chaos of my personality. The great clincher was the first LSD experience. While others had profoundly beautiful visionary experiences, or at least made claims to such, in my typically contrary hostile manner I had magnificent nightmares of indescribable dimensions. Deeply affected by the Vietnam War, my hallucinations consisted of napalmed Asian babies and I screamed out in outrage. It was quite an experience for the adults dealing with me as they tried to steer me away from the whole topic. In my mind it grew to paranoiac proportions of international significance. The more they tried to get me off the subject the more I viewed it as a fascist plot to keep my concern off of Vietnam…

A few years later, I heard of Jim Jones through students of his at the Ukiah Adult Education Night classes. All the young people in attendance raved about his class. I was at the high school one night with a friend and we decided to drop in the class for a visit. I must say I was very much unnerved when I found myself standing at the door, after class had started, peering into the window to discover a class packed wall to wall. I was ready to call it a day and go home. My friend was persistent and I entered the class with much trepidation and full anticipation of being physically tossed out of the room for one: being a hippy; two: disturbing the class with our late entrance. Neither one nor two occurred. Number three: Jim said, "Hello, how are you? We are so pleased to have you. Could someone get these young ladies a chair?" I sat down in amazement and gratitude. It was a shock to be treated like a human with respect and decency. I was very touched by his ability to find justice in every situation as he taught current events to a very mixed class ranging from rednecks to radicals.

One evening our home was further disrupted. My mom had recently separated from my dad after he moved his young girlfriend quite boldly into our house. I had just been kicked out of the house *again* by my dad. After a few weeks at a friend's house, I came back and was accepted back without tomatoes and rotten eggs hurled at me. Unfortunately my timing was bad. It was the same night that Mendocino County decided to make an election issue out of the drug traffic in the county. Our home was descended upon. I was in my bedroom and saw cars entering the driveway at high speed. Thinking it was more company, I pointed out that someone had just arrived. Someone shouted, "It's the fucking cops." I ran out to the living room to inform Jose of this new development...

At this point I found it expedient to go back to my room and stuff the bag of marijuana down my jeans. I came back to the dining room to see my dad struggling as they drug him out of the house. I screamed out in anger, "You can't take my dad away!" I tried to run after him and one cop grabbed me by the arm. I drug him through the dining room, the kitchen and out the back porch—struggling, fighting, kicking, and cursing. Another cop assisted him and they handcuffed me and drug me off to another car. I managed to get one handcuff off and eat the grass in the bag...

My dad in one car, the minor females in one and the minor males in another, we were all driven to Ukiah... On the way to Juvenile Hall, I admonished all the young ladies not to tell the pigs a thing. I must say we did a much better job than our weak-kneed brothers. We didn't say a word and two of them signed statements. We locked arms and refused to talk... I'll never forget the feeling of lying on the top bunk of the cell unable to sleep after they shut the damned door and one at a time, all the youngsters with families that had money were removed and sent home.

The charges were dropped against everyone but my dad. I believe that I was charged with resisting arrest, striking an officer, being a minor out of parental control, and being in a house where drugs were being used or sold... My dad was charged with selling marijuana to an undercover agent. It was election year for Sheriff Bartlomei and he played up this whole issue to the hilt, as if he had cleaned up the major drug traffic in the county.

In the months that followed I experienced one of the most painful events in my life. It's easy to make light of now, but at the time I was deeply affected and disturbed. The *Ukiah Daily Journal* took a little bit of fact and wove the most outrageous distortions that I could imagine. I was filled with an impotent rage that seemed to consume my personality. Already ostracized in the little provincial community, we became nearly totally outcast. I remember that I was not allowed to go to people's homes. The few times that I did it was under an actual assumed name! This was a new perspective for me as I had formerly been Girls Athletic Manager, Vice-President and President of the student body, and people had related to me as being among the "popular set." I was used to my peers looking up to me and had a rude awakening to the shallowness of such relationships.

I continued to go to Jim's night class and was amazed that he was concerned about my family's situation. One time in class he asked me if my father's business was suffering as a result of the bad publicity. The subject was a difficult one for me and a bit of pain must have flickered across my face. Jim immediately said, "Never mind, I don't want you to talk about it. I can see it is too painful for you to discuss." I was quite touched at that sensitivity, for it was *very* rare.

I became increasingly disturbed and quit attending night class. Jim continued to show concern and sent his associate minister, Archie Ijames, to my dad's trial. After Jose was sentenced to prison, Archie opened his home to Jose's girlfriend and she moved in with the Ijames family and began attending Peoples Temple. Eventually I began attending. I was intrigued by his social message but had an extremely difficult time adjusting to the religious vernacular and midwestern constituency. I had always had a great deal of independence as a child and had to adjust myself to the tight-knit community of Peoples Temple.

▓ *Henry Mercer* joined the Peoples Temple in 1973 when he was eighty-eight years old. He went to a Peoples Temple meeting in Philadelphia and followed them out to California. He and his sister eventually moved into an apartment in San Francisco with Hyacinth Thrash and her sister, Zipporah Edwards. Politically active all his life, Henry Mercer had been blinded by tear gas during a strike against Philadelphia's board of education.

I was born in Jessup, Georgia, April 3, 1885. I went to school to the sixth grade. My daddy died when I was thirteen years old and I had to go to work to help my mother. I considered then that there was something wrong at that young age because I knew that I seen the white kids had something that I just couldn't have. I seen the oppression of all people, white and black. When I was around sixteen years old I joined the Marcus Garvey movement and quite naturally started to learn a lot about the revolutionary struggle.

But to go back a bit first. One thing I can tell you. When I got to be a young man, I was working one night at the ice plant and a honkey picked me up in a car and said, "I just got to kill me a nigger tonight." And I was scared to death. He put a pistol to my head and drove all around. And he came back, he brought me back and he said, "Well, you're a good nigger, go ahead and go to work. You ain't the one I was looking for." That was in Georgia, Wayne County.

We used to go out and pick cotton. This was before I worked on the railroad, you know, to help along with the family because my dad wasn't making but a dollar and a quarter a day. There was four of us in the family to feed and he somehow or another managed to provide a place and pay for it. He worked in a freight house and I used to help pick cotton from the time I got out of school at two o'clock to into the evening. Cotton come in around the middle of August… I never saw a lynching but I saw it after it happened. It's an ugly looking thing… I went away from there. I stayed away twenty-six years and I went straight from Jessup to Philadelphia. All of us blacks used to keep guns… It was a terrible place, a terrible place. You were always in fear of your life and I was glad when I was big enough to leave. I can remember back and it's painful to think about. While I'm on it, a lot of us poor farmers had good livestock, horse and wagon, and had a crop, and then if you didn't leave, the whites would burn your house down. That way they took everything. A lot of poor fellows had to leave there by night with nothing but what they had on their back. One thing I can say, that we were all for one and one for all—we stuck together. That's what kind of kept it down. I don't know how many guys I shot, I don't know how many guys I wounded, but I know I got away from there…

One thing I always did hate—a sneak and a stool pigeon. I never did like a stool pigeon or a snitcher. I never was one myself. I wasn't an Uncle Tom myself and I hate that. I hate that, just like I hate a defector, a counterrevolutionary. I hate an anti-socialist and all that. I tell you I feel like going out and chewing them up when they do anything against the working class, against the poor people. Sometimes, I cry about it, the hurting things, to think about it—till Jim Jones came and rescued me. You don't know until you go through it. People say I'm a socialist. I'm a socialist. But they don't know. It takes more than you know to be a socialist. I got many a beating by the police. I beat many of them too—don't you think I didn't do that. I know many tricks about fighting in the revolution. In fact, I went to a revolutionary school for two years. I was designated to go to Moscow, but I didn't go.

I worked on the railroad. We were getting a dollar a day. I remember in 1910 the comet star, the star with the tail on it. Churches was full and everybody bordered the streets, most of the people was scared, they was afraid. The whites, they came out of the house and tell us all of a sudden that they weren't no better than us—and let's all get down and pray together, 'cause when the comet star touched earth it was going to set it on fire. I remember that real good.

In 1914, World War I broke out and at that time Germany was an empire and they had many colonies in Africa. I was working on the railroad and I didn't have to go. I was running the road at that time and we were doing a lot of defense hauling and I was even a part of the Liberty Bond Train.

In 1929, I joined the Unemployment Movement in Philadelphia. We got to have jobs, everybody was unemployed and nobody was employed and nobody knew what to do. There were many days I was hungry. There was many days I didn't have food to eat. They was giving us soup, watery soup, and we had to go to the station house to get it. During this time we were in line and some communists came along and distributed leaflets. I take one of the leaflets and read it and it said "meeting tonight," at a place they had in Philadelphia called 612 Brooklyn Street. And we went that night. There we had a discussion on strategy. We were going to organize the workers… The spring of 1930 it was, and sometime in the middle of May we met there with a hunger march. We carried around one hundred fifty of us to Harrisburg, Pennsylvania. But we had to struggle to get there. We were denied entrance to many towns. We negotiated and went through, and we went to Harrisburg and they wouldn't even give us a place to stay, they wouldn't rent a hall to us. We had a meeting the next day on the Capital Plaza. We had communists come from west of Pennsylvania, miners and different unemployed workers. At that time we had three hundred thousand people unemployed in Philadelphia and the government was not giving one nickel of relief, not one cent of relief. So we went and pressured the state and they gave us some form of relief. All channels are exhausted and that was the onliest way we could get anything, by pressuring the state government.

The Democratic Convention came off somewhere about 1931. Roosevelt came out, and in his speech he said, "One third of the people are unemployed." After he was elected he went to Congress and called for billions of dollars for the first work program that we had. It lasted about six months because the politicians stole all the money. And then they had little local relief programs in the states to try to tide us over. Had us working for our relief. What we did wasn't useful work. We'd dig stumps, clean up golf courses and such as that. Then came WPA. They worked ten thousand people in Philadelphia, it was the biggest project that we had. We had some miserable conditions on the WPA job. We decided we'd call a strike, and members were called out and singled out, the leaders were singled out as communists and they were immediately transferred away from the project to other projects that was much tougher. I was one. They transferred me to a stone quarry. Well, that was pretty hard work—I didn't have no experience about breaking stones. I worked there about eighteen months, and during that time I was in an accident and we didn't get paid for that.

Around 1939, I got a job at a naval yard but I never did sign the denial that I was a communist because I was a communist and I never did sign it. I was Chairman of the Propaganda Committee, and I had a tough time. If you was a Communist at that time, you had a tough time. After that, we had Joe McCarthy in the 1950s. They called us subversives and I was arrested for that, but we had a good law department and I came clear of that. I was arrested again. I was picked up again and they take me in and interrogate me. They called certain names and I didn't know nobody. I wouldn't talk…

I had other jobs and then I went to work for the Board of Education. During that time I was a union steward in the union and we got along pretty good. We had some terrible working conditions, where they worked women part-time. We demanded they work them eight hours. They claimed they couldn't work the women eight hours, so we had a meeting and decided to call a strike. That was around 1968. During this time I was doing pretty nicely. I was steward in the Union and we was having little skirmishes but no strikes. But it was at this time that we called this strike, and that's when I got it—I got my eyes blinded from tear gas.

When I got out of the hospital, I joined the Senior Citizen's Action Alliance. I worked in that from 1968 to 1973. And we done a lot of good…

In the winter of 1973 I was sitting down on the corner one night, and I had WCT radio station on and I heard this song and I heard this Peoples Temple Christian Church with Jim Jones as minister. I was impressed with the message. I called the station and asked for the address, and the man said, "The best I can do for you is Redwood City…" We took a bus to Redwood City and I called a taxi.

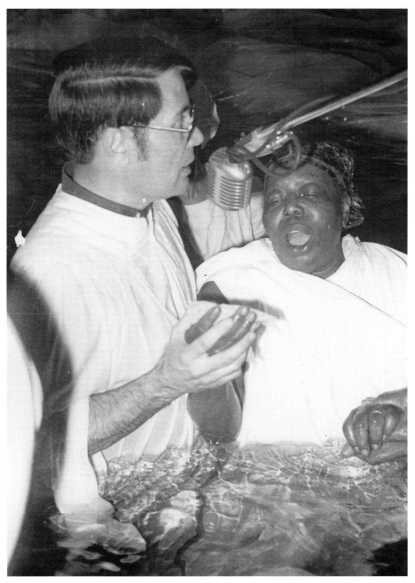

Above: Baptism in swimming pool at Peoples Temple church in Redwood Valley. Jim Jones's frequent use of sunglasses was noted in church bulletins: "Pastor Jones's sunglasses are ordinary sunglasses worn to reduce distractions during his meditations." MSP 3800

Top: Jim Jones with members of the choir behind him in July 1972. Message on the hand-lettered poster is "Pastor Jones wears a used choir robe to cover his worn attire. He buys no new clothes whatsoever!" MSP 3800

Below: Marceline Jones (*center*) with members at a church service in mid-1970s. MSP 3800

Jim Jones leaping off the stage at a church service in August 1972. MSP 3800

Jim Jones with Mr. Muggs, who was adopted by Peoples Temple in Redwood Valley in 1973. Mr. Muggs later accompanied Peoples Temple members to Jonestown. MSP 3800

Peoples Temple members in Redwood Valley. MSP 3800

Jim Jones at the podium with several glasses and a pitcher. He constantly drank beverages, especially cranberry juice, during Peoples Temple services, which often lasted for several hours. MSP 3800

JIM JONES
MIRACLE CRUSADE

Chicago

LOCATION:
TO BE ANNOUNCED

SATURDAY JUNE 26
SUNDAY JUNE 27

Philadelphia

THE BLUE HORIZON
1314 N. Broad St.
Philadelphia, Pa.
FRIDAY JUNE 18
SATURDAY JUNE 19

New York

AUDUBON BALLROOM
W. 166th & Broadway
New York, N. Y.
SUNDAY JUNE 20
MONDAY JUNE 21

Detroit

MASONIC HALL
500 Temple Ave.
Detroit, Michigan
THURSDAY JUNE 24
FRIDAY JUNE 25

Cleveland

WHK AUDITORIUM
5000 Euclid St.
Cleveland, Ohio
TUESDAY JUNE 22
WEDNESDAY JUNE 23

JIM JONES *is*
**REACHING
OUT TO
YOU!**
*PLAN TO
COME...
TELL ALL
YOUR
FRIENDS
& RELA-
TIVES!*

*It could
be the*
Turning Point
in their lives!

Peoples Temple included this flyer in their mail solicitations in 1973. MS 3800

HE'S ABLE
People's Temple Choir

Peoples Temple choir recorded this album featuring solos by Marceline and Jim Jones in 1973. The photograph on the cover was taken in front of Portals of the Past at Lloyd Lake in Golden Gate Park, San Francisco. MSP 3800

FACING PAGE:

Top: Peoples Temple church in Redwood Valley. Sign on the top of the building reads "Peoples Temple Christian Church and Youth Center Jim Jones Pastor." The church building included a swimming pool and an institutional communal kitchen. MSP 3800

Bottom: Peoples Temple members drove the "Greyhound-type buses" to services up and down the coast of California and across the country. Bus seven had a special compartment for Jim Jones. MSP 3800

Gathering of young adult members of Peoples Temple.
MSP 3800

The taxi driver took me around looking for the church. We went to the police station and I asked the desk sergeant about Peoples Temple. I called the secretary and they said they would come and get us, but I said, no, we will stay in a hotel and you can get us in the morning. When I got to the Temple, I got up to speak. I said I'd never liked preachers all my life, that I'd been a revolutionary for forty years and I never did like preachers, because they didn't want to do nothing but eat chicken and buy Cadillacs. The congregation went wild and cheered for a good while and I went back to sit down. Jim said to me, "You don't know how you thrilled my heart when you talked about the preachers." And I laughed. I seen some things I never seen before. I seen a dog up there with Jim and a cat came up and sat on [his] lap. I said, "My goodness, there's some love going around here, even the animals are loving you."

▓ Mendocino County has long been home to alternative communities. *Carol Stahl's* family belonged to one of them, the Christ's Church of the Golden Rule, a group started by Arthur Bell in the 1940s. The Golden Rule required its members to share all resources, live communally, and work for the church's businesses. Carol described the relationship between Peoples Temple and this well-established community until the groups split after a proposed merger fell apart in 1968. She also talked about her engagement to a member of Peoples Temple.

In 1965 I had just finished my education at San Jose State and had finished my training as an elementary school teacher. I had heard of Jim from my dad, who had told me about a young minister who had come from Indianapolis, who had led a group of people that my dad said were similar to ours—working for the betterment of mankind. The group I was with at the time was called Christ Church of the Golden Rule. I had been in that church from the time I was five years old. People in the church lived communally. So I have had experience with cooperative living all my life.

As I say, I was in the Golden Rule since I was very young. And, as I recall, my parents had been members of an organization called Mankind United prior to that, practically from the time of my birth. My dad used to go out in the streets and pass out pamphlets protesting World War II. They were quite active and it was a very unpopular stand to take. I recall them talking about the horrible things that Hitler was doing to the Jewish people. However, as they began to be attacked and people started saying they were subversives, I guess Arthur Bell, the leader of

Mankind United, felt that the only way to survive would be to form a church organization, that would be the only way to function. I guess there were several thousand people in the beginning who got together "projects." These were ranches, farms—where they raised produce and livestock for the people. They had hotels, motels, laundries that were run by volunteer help. All the services of the people were voluntary—no one worked an "outside job" for wages. Everything was collective. They were accused of being "Communists" and they began to crawl into a religious shell. Some of the leaders of the movement were attacked, sued, and the church was thrown into receivership and bankruptcy, and all the monies that were collected were given to the Bank's receivers, I guess you'd call them. They lost almost all of their property—at one time they owned property all up and down the State of California, and some in Oregon…

We wound up in California on one of the ranches, and I was there from 1963 to 1968 when I joined Peoples Temple. All my life I had grown up hearing that some day there would be other groups that we would merge with and work with, that were working toward the same goals that we were, of helping mankind—feeding the hungry, clothing the naked, etc. However, I did not see that we were really doing this. Yes, we were existing. We were eating. We had clothes on our backs. We did not individually have to worry about the bills being paid. But we were not branching out in any way.

When I met Jim Jones in 1965, he and a few people came to visit one of our meetings at Ridgewood Ranch, where we shared a few ideas… It was my understanding that Jim had tried to worship with various churches in the Ukiah–Redwood Valley area and he had been turned down by all of them because of the fact that they were an integrated church. The people at Ridgewood—Golden Rule—had told them that they could use the facilities there to hold their church services and meetings. And they did so for an extended period of time, about three years. In that time I grew to know and respect Jim more and more. Every spare moment that I had, I would be with the people. I had a lot of responsibilities with the Golden Rule. I was a member of the Board of Elders. I worked in the restaurant that we had, an income property, and also in the motel. I didn't have a lot of spare time. I had an invalid mother that I had to care for as well. But every spare moment that I had I spent with Jim Jones and other members of Peoples Temple. I saw that Jim was a man who genuinely cared for people and was trying actively to do something about relieving the misery of the poor.

The members of the church went around the community, visiting people who were sick, comforting them when there was a tragedy in the family, taking things to people if they were burned out in their home, seeing that if there was a death in the family, people had food taken to them. There weren't very many members of Peoples Temple at that time, maybe a hundred or so.

The background of the Golden Rule church was based on Christian Science faith, so I was familiar with Christian Science practitioners and faith healing. However, I was not too much aware of it personally, although my mother had seemingly overcome a lot of physical problems. She seemed like she was on the verge of dying many times, and with the help of meditations of practitioners, she seemed to come through a lot of things. I don't know. I don't understand that part of it. All during that time I had never actually seen Jim Jones heal anybody. I was more interested in the practical applications of Christ's teachings as I had been taught—feeding the hungry, etc. Though I had been reared with that belief, I had not actually become all that involved with that part of it, and this really intrigued me. Jim came to the Golden Rule very humbly, very open. They at first had their own separate services, although they invited the people from the Golden Rule to come and worship with them if they chose. However, it had been the policy of the Golden Rule never to visit other churches or become involved in their religious worship. Yet, some people did go periodically. I was one of those people.

On several occasions after they'd been there a while, members of the Board of Peoples Temple met with our Board and talked about the possibility of working together and of actually merging. Jim was very open to this. He even said that if they were threatened by his leadership, because he was very much respected and revered by his own people, he would step down. I could see why people thought so highly of him. But I could see that many of the leadership there who were up in years were very much threatened by this—by his youth, his obvious grasp of matters. I think that many of them had grown very complacent—I myself had grown complacent—too satisfied, too settled in the groove. I was comfortable. I didn't have any physical needs or wants. I know in the Golden Rule we didn't confront one another—it was kind of a peace at any price philosophy…

As I said, they were very threatened by Jim. I had become engaged to one of the members of the Peoples Temple, and we wanted to get married. On several different occasions my fiancée had gone with my dad and my stepmother to the Senior Elder to try and work out a way where we could get married and yet neither of us have to give up membership in our own church. And at this time we still had hopes that there would be a merging of the two groups, and it was even felt by some of us that our marriage would help bring this about. We were turned down, and one evening Jim and several other members came to one of the Wednesday night meetings that we held at the Golden Rule, and asked why we couldn't get married and still hold our separate memberships? One person got up and was very dogmatic. Either Richmond would have to give up his membership in Peoples Temple or I would have to give up my membership in the Golden Rule. And if I didn't like it, I could just leave. At that point Jim and the other members of the Temple got up and walked out, and said they would move their organ and other things out that evening. And they came back that night and did just that. I walked out with them.

We went down to Redwood Valley and had a meeting about what to do now that they had no place to hold their services. I decided at that time that I was going to move my things out that evening myself. And so several of them went back with me. My dad did not understand why I was doing this. He thought I should think it over. But I'd decided it was time I did some thinking for myself…

As the [Peoples Temple] church became more influential in the community, we began to have harassing phone calls. I know, I was called up in the night and called "nigger-lover," heavy breathing. I was told that Jim would be killed and other members of the church would be killed. There were shots fired at the church. They killed some of our animals, poisoned them. Strangled one cat. It became more and more evident that the feeling was more and more against black people and Jim Jones in the community. He caused people to think. You cannot be around Jim Jones and not think. And you either become hostile because he pricks your conscience or you begin to analyze and change your own way of doing things. You just don't remain complacent.

◼ *Cynthia Davis* recounted the history of her family's beliefs in witchcraft and Catholicism, shared stories about her bisexuality, and explained the changes in her political ideology since joining Peoples Temple in 1972.

I left Texas when I was twenty-one because of my mom—because of my mom, and my dad and myself. It was mostly my mom. She was religious and believed in stuff like witchcraft. She had a feeling that her relatives were trying to kill her and her immediate family… because of my grandmom's property. So, she decided she wanted to move.

My mom's belief in witchcraft started when she was a little girl. It's like a generation [thing] that people just pass down. Witchcraft was just one of them. My grandmom told all of her daughters certain things about witchcraft—things to watch out for that people are supposed to be able to hurt you with. It's like a protective thing that parents tell their children. A lot of black families—southern black families—believe in it. My mom told me about witchcraft when I was twelve years old. She told me a lot about it then. It was just a thing where parents try to protect their children. She would talk to me about it—tell me certain things that went on in her life, things that I should watch out for.

She had seen voodoo dolls and how people use them. She had seen people get sick behind witchcraft. She had seen the stuff that different people would vomit up. It was supposed to be things that poison would do to you. She had seen people just shrivel up and waste away to skin and bones. She had seen bloody masses come from people's mouths. It really puts a control on a person. I don't very well appreciate it now because it put quite a control on my life for a long time till I was twenty-three or twenty-four. In fact, I didn't get out of it myself until I joined Peoples Temple and actually started believing that no power was a great power—it was all just a religious, superstitious thing... She believed that the only way to get rid of this witchcraft was to do a heavy religious trip. If anything wrong happens, the only way to get rid of it was to go straight to church and pray.

Of course, there was a lot of rebellion because young people are not as religious—they're just not going to fall for it. My dad couldn't stand church either. He wouldn't go. They'd get in arguments all the time about it. It caused a lot of hell. So when this thing came up, my grandmother dying, of course her sisters and brothers they fight over money. She just figured that her sisters and brothers—about five or six of them—are trying to kill her and trying to kill me and my dad and my brother. So we just took off. We moved. My brother was already in the service. He was in California and he had asked that we come out there and join him anyway 'cause he liked it there. So we just decided to go ahead and move to California...

My becoming a lesbian was a very predictable thing. It came about as a result of the natural thing, the natural hurt thing that takes place when females interact with males. Women are brought up most of the time religious with customary male-female relationships. When you're eighteen, you get married and you live happily ever after. You raise a family and the whole trip. I'm not going to say I wasn't brought up like that. In fact, that's the same ideas and hopes and dreams I had. But when you get into relationships, of course you get hurt and most times I felt that relationships I got in, that's what happened—I got hurt...

It was funny the way I even started out in a lesbian life. It was strange. I dropped relationships altogether. It was unexpected. But there was this one young lady who was younger than myself who was very persistent... I hadn't expected I would do that. I just tried it you know. I enjoyed it. It was a new thing for me. She was more experienced at that thing because she had been a lesbian since she was about 14 years old. After getting into it, I liked it much better. I got a clear look at males and the games they play—the trips they put women through. I guess it was like going through a certain stage for myself. I became more hostile; I became a female chauvinist, a male-hater completely…

There are issues in this male-female thing that do not break down easily. Why, for instance, if women are brighter and more sensitive etc., aren't they more aggressive and acknowledged as leaders? To me, there is a reason for it. It's not the fact that women are as a whole scared or afraid to be in those positions or afraid to think [about] those positions or afraid to take that stand in life. But I think it's like—I've spoken of the generation thing. Something goes from generation to generation to generation like witchcraft. It's the same thing with women and religion. It's a customary thing you do. Like women go way back, as far as I'm concerned, in oppression. It's always been said, "It's a man's world…" There are some women that think they enjoy it. They're the kind of women that don't give a damn. They'd just rather let the men run the country or have the politics or have the businesses or be the doctors or be the lawyers or what have you. Then there are some women like today—they're trying. They're saying, "Damn this, we can be a better politician, a better driver, a better doctor, a better lawyer, a better teacher." And eventually women will have those positions. They will run things—that's the way I feel about it. But it takes time.

To me, it's just the way the world was set up from the beginning. But women, of course, have to change it. We don't have to *stay* that way, damn. They can change it if they will. If I know women, they're smart and they will.

Communism is the only way you can get equality. Communism—everything belongs to the working class and the working class have no segregation of women and men. It's just people. And under communism, heck yeah, you can do it…

For years, I've watched the women's movement… I never believed in it. I always thought it was a bourgeois trip. I always thought it was a bunch of middle class women that got together in these little jive meetings to discuss bullshit—taking off bras and beating up men. I always thought it was something they had to do besides having tea and cookies. They were bored so they got together and started talking about liberation, right? But I've never seen anything happen from it—all these unnecessary picket lines and these marches, newspaper interviews, and television interviews and I've never seen it change anything… The only time I've ever seen *any women liberated* was in this movement and the idea Jim Jones brought about…

▓ In January 1974, *Amanda Poindexter's* ninety-ninth birthday was featured on the front page of the Temple's occasional publication *Family Good News*:

> All the gang was there to hear our precious senior citizen EVER REJOICING sing *99-1/2 Won't Do*—an original composition—at her birthday party the other day. She was as lively and rejoicing as ever: her name is more than appropriate! She definitely gets the Good News nomination for the "Senior Power" title. We all thank her for the tremendous inspiration that she has been since she came to the family from Philadelphia over two years ago.

> Ever Rejoicing was the name she took when she belonged to Father Divine's Peace Movement, based in Philadelphia. Other Temple members, such as Love Joy and Heavenly Love, also kept their names from those days. Ever Rejoicing's family history in America began in slavery.

My parents were slaves in Halifax County, Virginia. My mother died in 1936. She tells about getting whippings. She was fifteen when Lee surrendered. She cried when she told about it. My father was a house nigger slave. The master wouldn't even allow the people to pray. They had to have their prayer meeting in secret. Once they saw a man praying and they nailed his tongue to a tree. They had to turn an iron pot upside down to catch the sound to keep the prayer meetings a secret. Had to be careful in those times.

My family moved to Philadelphia around 1890. I went to work as a domestic worker for years and years.

I learned to walk when I was seven months old. I remember I was born psychic. I could see spirits. One morning when Dad went to the stable, my mother dressed me in my first pair of shoes. There were brass tips on the toes. I saw all kinds of things. Worked on a farm from time to time when I was twelve. My dad was a drunkard—the master taught him to drink. He grew tobacco and sugar cane. We got nothing and worked hard. I wanted to leave. My sister was the first one to go to Philadelphia. There was no money to go to school—too far, too cold. Learned on my own to read and spell. My first job was for a dollar a week taking care of a woman, washing her dishes. Next job was two dollars a week. Had to work for seven people. Plenty of wash. Women wore blouses with ruffles and changed them two or three times a day.

I remember back on the farm, the pots hanging on the chimney. Before my dad, Peter Poindexter, died, he and Mother went back down to Virginia. I worked all the time. Couldn't save any money at all. When my sister was sick, I had to help her, take care of her. Went from one domestic job to another.

I got married. I don't know why. I didn't love him. After five months, I left. He was a cabinetmaker, but lazy. He wanted me to work. Made me take a job as a laundress. I'm not much at lying, but I tricked him. I told him I had a job for both of us, and he sent my things to Massachusetts.

I joined the Peace Mission in 1942. Was in Father Divine movement for nearly thirty years. But he didn't take people in to stay overnight…

I was brought up in Baptist church, then Methodist. They lied and stole so much that I left. People who will do that, it will sneak up on them someday. Churches are full of liars, thieves and hypocrites. I saw a preacher steal money to build a church. But he never finished paying for it. The chairs in the church—he made people pay for them several times over. Used the money on himself. I finally just left altogether. They were paying off that church for eighteen years! All of those churches—they were the same.

Dick Tropp and his sister, Harriet S. Tropp, who also used the name Sarah Tropp, joined Peoples Temple in 1970. Dick Tropp oversaw many of the Temple publications, especially the development of the *Peoples Forum*, which Temple members distributed to hundreds of thousands of homes in the San Francisco Bay Area in 1976 and 1977. In his role as an educator, he worked with many of the students in the Temple-sponsored college dormitories. His writing efforts included drafts of a biography of Jim Jones and a history of Peoples Temple.

This is a very brief, sketchy rundown.

I started out in the Bedford-Stuyvesant, grandson of Jewish immigrants from Eastern Europe. Lower middle class upbringing in suburbs on Long Island, and did very well in school. Deep interest in music, and studied cello from age nine. Went to University of Rochester where I majored in English and comparative literature and developed intellectual interests. Studied with Norman O. Brown, Hayden White, other excellent teachers. Interests in existentialist philosophers, drama, history of ideas, mysticism. Graduated with highest honors. Went to Europe on a travel scholarship. Lonely, depressed a lot, and felt that all I had learned was somehow an exercise in futility. I was seeking for something else. All intellectual friends, everything, seemed to be poised at the verge of total failure. Studied Beckett with

Ihab Hassan, which had deep influence over me. Consumed with idea of apocalypse, and found my life directionless. Tried to pursue academic route at Berkeley, 1965–66 on a Wilson Fellowship. I was supposed to go "to the top" in my field, but somehow I had profound dissatisfaction with it all. I equated academic life with death. After I received Masters, I had been experimenting with psychedelic drugs, had drifted into the "hip" culture of Berkeley, and my outlook became that of a confused radical Utopian. I lived on several communes, all disappointments.

I was torn between several poles: intellectual, social conscience (I was a participant in civil rights demonstrations and marches, and by the mid-sixties I was attracted by revolutionary ideas), transcendence (the urge to overcome, to become "enlightened," to have supreme-awareness type experiences). Also hedonistic side of personality that kept me from concentration anywhere. I found no people around me who I could relate to—they were either in one world or another—I was in several (I had always felt myself looking for a *synthesis* of those "worlds" and reference points—that was a controlling metaphor during those years). In late 1967, I accepted a teaching position at Fisk University in Nashville. I became involved in everything from radical politics, supplying some of the kids there with good marijuana from New York, teaching very offbeat (for Fisk) classes that got me in trouble with the faculty and administration. I ran in a lot of circles, and finally, when the year was up, the administration decided that they had enough of me.

I had planned to leave anyway. Back to Berkeley to study classical Indian music with Ali Akbar Khan. The other pole. Music—culture—search for transcendence. I was seeking for something. Berkeley was a nirvana supermarket, and I was a shopper. Very unhappy. Taught part-time at Merritt College, ran around with all kinds of losers. Couldn't get a handle on my life.

I was accepted in a teaching post at Santa Rosa Junior College (back to the nipple of knowledge). But a few weeks before I was to start, I went through some kind of change—I again feared that I would "die" in the college. I made a spur of the moment decision to move to Mendocino County and mine jade with a friend of a friend. My girlfriend and I settled in Redwood Valley in a cabin in late 1969. The jade business lasted two months. I was unemployed, drifting. Looking for people with whom to buy land and start a community. I had some plans—fairly Utopian. But never could seem to find the right people. They were either too far one way or another, yet at the same time (typically) I was too far from them. I met Jim Jones in the spring of 1970.

In Peoples Temple I have found the synthesis I was always looking for, personified in Jim Jones. At once a spiritual teacher, a down-to-earth human being, a person who represents to me the Nietzschean "overman" who builds that bridge of transition between the human animal and the human being. And who is not one to transcend for himself, but who has sacrificed himself for the cause of human overcoming on a myriad of levels. I have never met any person who brings those seemingly disparate and mutually exclusive worlds together. He is a psychic technician, a person with a strong, extraordinary imaginative/mind/power who uses that power for good. I could go on for a long time.

To be brief, I have found a place here to serve, to be, to grow. To learn the riddle of my own insignificance, to help build a future in the shadow of the apocalypse under which I felt I was always living. All these controlling metaphors that were kicking around my subconscious during the 1960s have again been reshaped, synthesized. I took a job at Santa Rosa Junior College in 1972, teaching what I wanted to, though my work for the cause has been most consuming and has become absolutely central to my life. When I met Jim Jones I was a sick, directionless, impossibly thwarted human being. My talents were going to waste. Well, that's about enough for this sketch.

Coda: I look back on the past as if to another world, a dead and dying world. I could have achieved success in the knowledge-empire. I was unable, however, to fit in there. I wanted something else, something *more*. All the analysis, ideas, insights, etc.—somehow, underneath, there was an emptiness. Life was inane. I ventured out beyond that and almost was lost. But I had no choice. I felt that I had to move out, keep exploring, wrestle with the sense of futility. I knew somehow that there was light at the end of the tunnel. Now I am in a struggle that consumes my time and energy. I feel very grateful to be working with a man who I consider to be a higher, more evolved type of being. A savior, in the most profound sense of that much-abused word (1 can think of no other off hand). I don't mean this in some cheap "religious" sense, but in terms of the evolutionary/spiritual direction of humanity. The conditioning I received as an intellectual had a lot of influence on the development of my ego-structure. Sometimes I look back. I sometimes look at things in terms of the parameters of the "dead" world. But a new center of gravity has been established in my life—and, to my great relief and happiness, it is not *me*.

■ *Annie Moore* joined Peoples Temple in 1972 after her high school graduation. Her older sister, Carolyn Layton, had been a member for four years. Annie lived in Temple-sponsored dormitories until she graduated from nursing school.

From childhood up to junior high school, I was what I would call "protected," although my parents were liberals and open to the rights of all—despite their race, creed, or color, whether prisoners, homosexuals or mentally ill. It took me until the eighth grade to start really realizing what the world was all about. This was when I began to really think and notice how unhappy much of the world was. I began to question the actions of those adults that I had looked up to. There were different people I knew who had committed suicide and others who were killed in car accidents. I knew there was a war going on in Vietnam and was involved in war protests and fights with the "cowboys" at school over this. By the ninth grade, I was totally confused, lonely, bored, and I began experimenting with drugs—although my parents never knew about it. I lacked self-confidence so much and had such a poor self-image that I thought about different ways to commit suicide. I put on an act through most of high school pretending I was crazy, doing outrageous things like making faces at teachers and following different people I disliked acting like a chimpanzee. I did anything to cut the boredom and the only way I could handle it was by making a joke out of life.

At age sixteen, I worked in a burn unit at Children's Hospital in Washington, D.C. for the summer. The children needed someone to play with since their parents worked or didn't care to come and visit them. There was so much pain in their faces from the hell they went through!… After working there I was never the same. I returned to high school the next year. More than anything, I wanted to do something with my life that would be helping people… but after mixing with the same bunch of friends—some of whom were shooting heroin, and others who were involved in various crimes—I selfishly planned to commit suicide at some time. I had no one I could express what I really felt about anything to and I was upset that the boys at school who liked me were always the creepiest creeps you could find.

Finishing my high school years in a university town, I had grown to hate intellectuals, because they were all a lot of hot air and no action. This is why. Whenever I was on a project to care for prisoners' children while the wives visited their husbands, or when I was tutoring minority children in their schoolwork, the intellectuals could always find a reason why they could not help. But they always had plenty of time to talk about the world's problems and sermonize about what *should* be done.

So, due to my eccentric hate for intellectuals and school, I refused to go on to college. My mother wanted me to be an artist or musician, but I hated them too. I thought they were all so phony and egotistical. So I had no plans, was totally confused, and poured an entire bottle of codeine pills in my mouth preparing to swallow them. I don't know why I stopped, but I did—and spit them all out into the toilet. Days later, my sister who was in Peoples Temple invited me to visit. I found people who were friendly, mixing all races together, working in a cooperative setting. The people were not phony and seemed for real. They took no drugs and still seemed to enjoy themselves. So, not having anything else to do with myself, I came. Jim told me that I could be helpful in the group, that I was talented and could teach others or even go to school and make something of myself. He convinced me it was not right to commit suicide and that I could be useful and gain happiness by helping others. It was he and the support of Temple members that helped me though nurse's training, which I had adamantly refused to attempt at first. I found that even though I hated intellectuals and didn't like the schools I'd been to, I had nothing against learning. Now I've been an R.N. for three years and my life is fulfilling.

■ There were many extended families in Peoples Temple. *Shabaka Baker's* family attended services in the early 1970s and then left the church for a while, returning later. This was not unusual, especially for families who had relatives still involved in the Temple. In his recollections, he mentioned watching *Roots*, a popular 1977 television mini-series based on Alex Haley's best-selling book about his family's African ancestry.

Well, ever since I was small I was always a quiet person, so that always made me feel kind of left out. I grew up in the small town of Pomona. Nothing ever went on there and I was always excessively bored. I never had many friends—one or two maybe, if I'm lucky. I didn't know too much about drinking and smoking. So all I did was watch TV and eat plums… I was spoiled and got my feelings hurt easy.

What was really a put-down was that everyone in my family had at least one or two baby pictures except me. I would bother my mother from time to time asking her, "Why don't I have a baby picture?" All she ever showed me was a picture when I was about four years old, but that never did satisfy me. The more I bugged her, the more angry she got, so I just left it alone. Still I never forgot that when I asked to see my baby picture, she said, "Oh honey, you do have a baby picture" and pulled out that picture of me when I was four. Finally she came to me one day and explained why I had no baby picture. She said, "Well son, I was going through a lot of changes when you were born—you understand, don't you?" "Yeah, I understand. I didn't want to see myself anyway." Well, I soon went through that era in my life, but still, I was bored.

Sometimes when I would come home from school and watch the school students walking, chatting with their friends, I would always envy the fun they had. It was hard for me because I was so quiet... But when I came to Peoples Temple I really found friends. I didn't expect people to like me, simply because I looked down on myself too much. But when I came to the Temple I got confidence in myself—self-pride.

I had a lot of fun at the Redwood Valley Peoples Temple. I would just feel the love and solidarity and I wanted to stay there forever. But when I got back to Pomona, it was like going on another planet. More Mexicans were moving in from Tijuana. Blacks and Mexicans were always fighting. At first, it was the whites vs. the blacks. Now two other races were fighting. It made me sick. Then when it seemed like the Mexicans were winning (and finally they did), everybody wanted to be Mexican.

I would have never come to the Temple if it weren't for Chris Lewis, my uncle— but in my heart, he was my daddy. When my dad, Bill Baker, wasn't getting along with my mom, Barbara Baker, one day he just got in his car and drove away. I didn't see him for about three years. Well, my mom didn't own the house. She had no job and didn't know how to drive. With four young children on her hands, she didn't know how to do it on her own. When Chris and my grandmother found out, they quickly moved in and helped. Chris was a gangster then, so he gave my mom lots of money.

My grandmother took care of us and taught my mom how to drive. I disrespected my grandmom very much. I took my hostilities out on her simply because she was old. When she got sick and ready to die, I started to realize what I did— how I disrespected her. So before she died, I just had to show that I really did love her.

My granddad, I never knew him. He died of cancer before I was born. All I know is he was from Trinidad. His name was Rudolf Alexander Lewis. He was a very handsome man from the pictures and participated in many riots in New York. He and his wife and three children, Barbara, Ruthann and Chris, moved to L.A. in 1945 into my great-grandmom's three-story house. Inherited from my grandmom, Chris was always outstanding. Barbara loved to party. Ruthann was the kind searching for Beverly Hills and she got it, too. She worked at a job that I would have hated to be at. She worked in a prison. My mom worked as a pre-school teacher. She was put through a lot of hell because of racism and she wouldn't take no shit from her fellow workers—white. It would have been easy for her to have asskissed, because she was mopping and scrubbing floors before she got the job. But she didn't sell out and she got fired. She took it to court because it was a conspiracy. She didn't win, but everyone in that preschool will never forget the hell she put them through. She was the best teacher and all the kids called her Teacher Baker.

Chris was a gangster and hooked on heroin till he came to Peoples Temple. When I lived with them, it was still far away from the Temple and it was hard for me coming from a loving society back to a hateful one—when I moved from Redwood Valley Peoples Temple back to Pomona. I started getting into fights and was expelled from school. Sometimes I would smoke about six packs of Winstons. I would rip off wine and beer. I just started throwing my life away... Then finally, my dad came back and he took us on trips. That fulfilled my life a little bit but not enough. I was looking for Peoples Temple once again, which I had left two years before. When I finally went back after two long years, my patterns changed overnight. I started to sing for Peoples Temple members. Once again, I had meaning to my life. My mom promised she would never leave [Peoples Temple] again...

Oh and by the way, my name wasn't always Shabaka. I changed it from Shawn when I saw *Roots*.

Letter to Jim Jones
Marceline Jones
June 8, 1970

In 1969, Jim Jones began an affair with Carolyn Layton, a high school teacher who had joined Peoples Temple in Redwood Valley the previous year. He did not conceal their relationship from his wife or from his children. Carolyn gave birth to their child, Kimo Layton, also called Jim-John, in January 1975.

Jim

As the time approaches for our 21st wedding anniversary, it seems appropriate to take inventory of our lives together. In one more year, I will have spent half my life with you. It is the only part of my life that counts. In that time I've known great joy and great sorrow. It has been my love for you that has tempered all things and made the good and the bad melt to compose a beautiful harmony.

This time of the year I remember, especially, the time of Stephan's birth. It followed so appropriately the death of a child. I experienced the extremes of emotion at that time—Extreme sorrow and extreme happiness. Most important—you were there. At that time, I had some of the idealistic anticipation that is characteristic of the young. I'm different now. Now—as I live one 12 hours at a time—I take time and am able to enjoy the small things. While I count on nothing for the future, I am able to enjoy the present more and, I think, put things more in this proper perspective. If I have no future with you, I'm grateful for today. But more about the things I remember. I remember our days together before we married. The hours you sat by my bed when I had infectious mononucleosis. I remember our wedding night and the days that followed with Humphrey Houdini. Our lunches and the maple-centered peanut clusters. I remember the foreign films we saw in Bloomington, the hours we spent at the golf course studying with Shirle and how she used to warn us of any approaching snakes. And there were our visits to the church where you so courageously told them of hypocrisy. Years have gone by and I remember the hundreds of things that occurred in our struggle to help make this a better world. How much fun we've had. In the beginning, in your drive to make it, you drove hard. I understand. I remember clearly when you began to relax and live and be tender with me. My love for you deepened. We had trips to Chicago. It seemed then that you even enjoyed the trips. I remember eating in a certain cafeteria and how we enjoyed watching and discussing the people. How we dreamed and planned. Many of the dreams have come true. Our beautiful children were conceived in those dreams. I'll never forget the day we landed in Mexico City and our experience there, staying in the Metropol Hotel. There we lost Stephan and it was there that baby Jim was such a hit. Then there was the day we landed in Sao Paulo, Brazil. How dejected I felt. Remember, as we were leaving the airport, we looked at each other and simultaneously started to sing the song that we heard at our wedding, "I'll be loving you always."

There was one milestone in our relationship that I've never shared with you. It happened in Rio de Janeiro—the evening I set out to meet you and got lost. I was hours late. When I arrived, you were visibly shaken. Would you believe that until that moment it had never occurred to me that losing me would bother you much. You had always been so strong, self-reliant and surrounded by people willing and able to meet your needs that I never really felt that I was important. As a matter of fact, your tendency to pull or almost force others into your life indicated to me that I had in some way disappointed you and had not met your need. This incident in Brazil gave me an inkling that maybe I was a little special. However, later I rationalized and decided that you were shaken then because I happened to be the only one there. I know now that you did care.

I could remember and remember. There is no end. In all my remembering, I must give most thanks to what I have learned in the past year. At times I don't know what is best for you. But—I do know you care. Regardless of who else you might care for, thank you for including me. I'm sorry for the times that I made you feel unloved. In my frustration as I tried to measure up but never quite doing it, I thought, I struck back in unkind ways. I'm grateful for the chance to prove my love to you. Thank you for your kindness and understanding. I don't know about tomorrow but today I give thanks for each moment I share with you.

Marcie

Holographic will
Marceline Jones
May 25, 1974

To Whom it May Concern:

In the event of my death, I Marceline M. Jones, would like for Carolyn Layton to take over the mothering responsibilities of my children. I would, in fact, hope she could move into the house and fill any void my absence might leave.

from a sermon in Redwood Valley
Jim Jones
1973

Jim Jones often referred to the income disparity in America in his arguments against capitalism and traditional organized religions. The following remarks from one of his sermons were recorded in Redwood Valley in 1973.

If there were no rich, no poor, if everyone were equal, religion would be soon to disappear. People only develop religion when they're unhappy with this world. But if this world were equal, if everything was equal, every opportunity—all of the land facilities, all of the health facilities, all of the food, every beautiful thing of this earth was available to all—people would soon lose their religion. And there would be no racial differences if everyone was equal. There would be no room for race. Race is developed because the rich want someone to do their slave work, servant work, and the black people just happened to be the slaves of this generation. In other ages, it was the Spanish, the Greek, the Italians, or the Indians, Chinese. Chinese were coolies and servants. It just so happens that the most recent slaves in America were black. But slaves are created because the rich need someone to do their dirty work. So racism is an out picture—is a result—direct result, of separation between people based on the ownership of property. I do not believe in private ownership of property. I believe that all property should be held in common. Just like this church belongs to all of us. Just like the lands out here, the fruit, everything is shared by all of us. Now, it's a small example. You can't even realize how beautiful that is. In certain countries of the world, a factory, for instance, will be owned by all the people.

Now, the factory downtown here, that's a major factory here, is a Masonite factory. It makes twelve million dollars a year for its owner, who never comes here. He's called an absentee landlord. He travels around on yachts, lives in luxury. He's a racist bigot. And he takes all this money. These poor workers, many in our church who work there, breathe the dust, don't have the advantages they need, and that money's all drained out to the rich owners… If that twelve million dollars was taken out of that factory by the people—it's done in certain places in Europe—the people own the factory, so around the factory will be all kinds of beautiful apartments, swimming pools, hospitals, doctors' free clinics, dental free clinics, schools, fine houses and lovely shrubs, and lovely gardens, because the people get all the profits and around every factory is a beautiful, beautiful community. There's enough money that comes out of that one factory to give everyone a home in this valley. So that's what we mean—we do not believe that the rich should be entitled to own things that they do not use. No one should be able to get anything out of something unless they put labor in it. Labor is the thing that makes the world go. It's the laborers of the world that gives everyone everything they have here. Somebody had to sweat to give us lights tonight…

Labor should get the full result of his work. That isn't to say that every person should get exactly the same wage. Maybe, for a while, there would have to be differentials. There would have to be slight differences to motivate people. Someone get a little bit more… We're not saying that everyone here should necessarily be paid exactly the same, although that would be ideal. I could be paid the same, even—if I had to do fifteen hours of work, and someone else in here was crippled or weak and couldn't do it, and they only do an hour's work, I'd be glad to work fifteen hours and have no more home, no more car, no more food than they did. I could gladly work in a society without being motivated by salary or special benefits.

I'm so purely socialistic and some of my family is so purely socialistic, some of the members of this glorious Temple are so purely socialistic, that you'd be glad to work to see that everyone had the same kind of house, the same kind of cars. Well, if you wanted your car painted differently, that'd be all right. You know, we're not talking about the same color, and exactly the same pieces of furniture… People are so afraid of socialism. They're so terrified. They say, "What'll it do to us?" Why you poor people. The people—the average man in the street, even the small grocery owner, the small businessman—if the money of this country were actually shared, there would be approximately one hundred and ten thousand dollars income for every person in America…

If you've got money equalized, and there was no real rich and no real poor, you'd have no racism. You'd have no religion. Because people only make heavens because this is so much a hell. They can't stand to look at this place. So they project a heaven out there that they got to go to—because they can't stand the earth—because the earth is in the hands of the robber-baron rich. It's in the hands of the capitalists. And they're poor, so they create a religious song. There was no heaven, like they sung about. The poor black people in the fields, they had to sing—"you got shoes, I got shoes," because they were going barefooted. And the terrible rocks and the thorns were penetrating their feet, and they had to develop something that would give them hope. They knew they'd never get any shoes off of the white master, the rich owner. They'd never get it. So they developed a religion that said by and by, "you got shoes, I got shoes, all God's children got shoes." It's a pitiful song. It comes out of the people that are poor… Heaven was created by poor people that were working cotton fields and working in mines and living in hell, so they had to create a golden city somewhere. They had to dream, because they knew they'd never get anything out of this earth. So religion is a dark creation of those who are oppressed, those who are in bondage.

Salute to Compatriot Don
Early 1970s

Peoples Temple sponsored communal college dormitories and often paid members' tuition expenses. The students lived, worked, and studied together. In this letter they congratulated a fellow Peoples Temple member for becoming the first African American to be hired by the Masonite Corporation, a manufacturing plant in Ukiah.

Dear Compatriot Don,

We students of the People's Temple College Dormitories salute you as a representative of this principle and the fact that you have made history by becoming the first Black worker to work at Masonite Corporation in Ukiah, California. A great responsibility is upon you, but we students want you to know that we stand behind you. You are part of the Vanguard of things to come, of a new day! As the first Black worker in this factory—it is you who will be a catalyst to heighten the consciousness of the workers around you to the Truth that all workers, Black and white, have a common goal. At this time they are reactionary racists for the most part but because of people with dedication and courage as yourself this will soon be changed. Our thoughts, our hopes, and our support is with you.

"Reflections on Leaving the Temple"
Vera Washington
November 2003

In 1973, a group of college-aged members of Peoples Temple decided to leave the church. Several of them had grown up in the church and were leaving their families as well as their community. They moved out of the Temple-sponsored dorms, communal homes, and their families' homes. Jim Jones's angry reactions when people left the church were well known to the membership. He and other Peoples Temple leaders would pressure the families of those who left to talk them into returning. Jim Jones often prophesied that people who left his church would come to great harm without his constant protection. Many members who left felt that they were breaking free from a community that was becoming increasingly oppressive.

In her reflections written thirty years after she left Peoples Temple, Vera Washington described her experience of the Temple in the early 1970s and what it was like to be part of this group, who became known as the "Gang of Eight."

When I was a first-year college student, I started attending Peoples Temple services. I met members of the Temple when they came to a Sunday worship service at our church in the Western Addition district in San Francisco. I was impressed by Jim Jones' down-to-earth "Just Keeping It Real" type attitude. I was from the South and had been active in the Civil Rights Movement, especially during the voter rights drives which were in full swing during the summer. Jim Jones was not just paying "lip service" to the cause but was actively promoting interracial lifestyles. This was all very impressive to me, so much so that I joined the Temple.

The early years were primarily intriguing. We were introduced to dormitory style living and sharing in a communal atmosphere. The college students benefited from the cohesive environment and were considered the pride of Jim and the Temple members.

We continued in this blissful period until about 1972. Then changes in the hierarchy of the Temple became defined, and the gentle atmosphere became a bit more controlled and less accommodating. The "teaching" sessions gave away to confrontational and sometimes moderately violent episodes. This created a tense and uneasy feeling among the congregation.

The students absorbed all of this. We were encouraged to spy on one another and turn each other in. Some of us decided that something was going terribly wrong, and we felt the loving teachings and considerate attitude that we had been taught as appropriate behavior were all being eroded. Jim appeared to be guided in his primary decision-making by a small elite group of what we considered high intensity egotistical people. He seemed to lose sight of his earlier goals and instead set out to acquire as much wealth as possible. He forced everyone to live communally and turn in all liquid assets. Mandatory tithing was to be 15% of your gross income. This left very little for daily expenses, and our requests to the Temple for the necessities of life grew into a disturbing dependency.

In 1973, eight members of the core group of college students secretly planned an escape and successfully pulled it off! We wrote a letter to Jim explaining our reasons for leaving and urging him to recapture both the ideals he had once espoused and the leadership example he had once modeled. We only hoped that others would garner whatever mental strength they had left and follow our lead.

from the Gang of Eight's letter to Jim Jones
1973

Jim:

Let us say that our departure has nothing to do with you. To us, you are the finest socialist and leader this earth has ever seen. We plan to contact you and, if you see fit, work with you, not staff. We have nothing to say to or with staff,

Several people have come to different ones of us with doubts about you, staff, Peoples Temple goal and money used. Those that have expressed doubts about you felt guilty, worthless and scared. We've told them all to write you and explain these feelings, because we didn't agree and didn't know how to help them. Most of them said, and we quote, "staff will only use it against us." To put it mildly, there are many people that hate staff with a passion. You know as well as we, if leadership is dishonest, if leadership is aloof and sacred from the common people, if leadership has a white attitude, a movement will be crippled if not destroyed. From our observation and dealings with Peoples Temple members, they have faith in you—only you.

You said that the revolutionary focal point at present is in the black people. There is no potential in the white population, according to you. Yet, where is the black leadership, where is the black staff and black attitude…

New white upper middle class folk seem to be trusted and treated better than black folk who have proven their loyalties through the years. There's never been one black person who's come into Peoples Temple and put on staff right away...

Why are there no black men or women with a revolutionary attitude coming into Peoples Temple? For the past 6 years all staff have concerned themselves with have been the castrating of people, calling them homosexual, sex, sex, sex. What about Socialism? Why isn't it top priority? If you say it is, how does 99½% of Peoples Temple manage to know zero about Socialism?

There's no revolutionary teachings being taught the way it use to. At one time you told us to read. Yet, staff came in the night to steal books from those who had them.

Take a look at what the youth group used to be and what it is now. Before, they planned, they were united and they were aware of capitalism as opposed to Socialism. Today, they're dumb when it comes to capitalism and Socialism, they hate going to all church meetings, they don't go to choir rehearsal, there's no youth group. Why?

When the college students held socialist meetings, not one young person left the group. There was unity. The college meetings were discontinued—ever since the college dorms have been going downhill...

To regress a bit, it is our feeling that staff have wiped out progressive and revolutionary thought. Peoples Temple members are expecting to enter a cave or go to some isolated part of another country—the bomb falls—they emerge and pow, paradise. This would never be the state of mind if the realism of supporting and believing in Socialism were understood. With this we feel some of us were kept from staff (by staff) because our ideals were and are too progressive and black. Anybody with a mind to be active concerning Socialism is put down, called a queer and big revolutionary in a degrading manner. Why?

We know you have far too much on you and have to rely on staff for facts etc. This puts you in a vulnerable position, because staff lies and their personal prejudices are given to you instead of fact. We've witnessed it as well as experienced it. How can one judge or be objective about something they fear. The staff, being uppity white folk, fear blackness, they fear what some of us had to offer, they fear the consequences of a do-it-now philosophy, they fear action.

We're told we're not ready—we need more money—we have to be closer. Well, Peoples Temple is a multi-million dollar church, and there's nothing being done to bring people closer. Hugging each other in services will not do it.

Male Chauvinism is used every other word. When this world is in the condition it's in, why be trivial? Of course, male chauvinism exists; however, it's over-emphasized. The male population at Peoples Temple have been saturated with the word and with people that use it. Again staff is responsible, they set the example...

In closing, let us bring to light one more situation. Jan Wilsey and Christine Lucientes came to Peoples Temple at the same time. Christine is put on staff, even though she shows more suicidal tendencies—runs away when confronted. Jan is at the doors every meeting doing her job. Christine flunks out of school, gives the church a bad name at SRJC [Santa Rosa Junior College] Nursing School. However, she's white and makes staff.

The eight of us believe in historical materialism. We feel that you came to the people giving them the greatest reason to live, the greatest reason to die, the greatest reason to fight—Socialism (we have another name for it). However, you can't do it all, you can't move unless your followers realize the necessity to shape history themselves. This is again where staff has failed. They are for the most part white egotistical people maintaining a hierarchy. Not allowing you to take the reins and go ahead full steam...

We will not talk against Peoples Temple to anyone, because of you and a few innocent people may be hurt.

You're the one that showed us the way, you're the one that boldly challenged capitalism and put a vision in our hearts, you're the one that proved to us that nothing is impossible. This is exactly how we feel—nothing's impossible... We want it known by you and staff that we don't believe in religion, we don't believe in God, we don't believe in reincarnation, we don't believe in impossible. We are not concerned with the beginning, the end or the hereafter. We are only concerned about today.

from a sermon given in Philadelphia
Jim Jones
mid-1970s

Jim Jones continued to challenge his audience's views about the U.S. government and capitalism. The following remarks from one of his sermons were recorded in Philadelphia in the mid-1970s.

You say, "I'm not a nigger." Sittin' back there, you're light. Oh, yes, you're a nigger.

I'm a nigger. I'm a nigger until everybody is free. Till everybody that's treated niggardly is free. I am a nigger. I don't care if you're an Italian nigger, or you're Jewish or an Indian, the only people that are getting anything in this country are the people that got the money, baby...

I've prophesied the date, the hour, the minute and the year they're gonna put people in this country in concentration camps. They're gonna put them in gas ovens, just like they did the Jews. They've started at Watergate, and they've told you, in the paper today, that we have been lied to at Cambodia, that we've bombed the wrong people, that we've killed innocent children, that you were lied to, and they're just seeing how much the people care. And if you don't resist, if you don't rise up and demand honest government—it's not going to be long, if we don't let the government be upon his shoulders, that they're gonna put you in the concentration camps that are already in Tule Lake, California, Allentown, Pennsylvania, near Birmingham, outside El Reno, Oklahoma. They've got them already, Title II of the McCarran Act, they still have the concentration camps, they did it to the Japanese, and they'll do it to us if we don't quit preachin' this pie-in-the-sky—You say, "It won't happen. Won't happen. Won't happen."

All right now, you brace yourself. Senator Kennedy's talked about, in Massachusetts, some Italian, Greek and German old ladies that's been experimented on, with government money, just because they were in nursing home, their brains has been cut on, without consent. Black children have been sterilized, all the way from Alabama to Carolina, against their will. The prisons—a doctor in our church, on Wednesday last, told of all the experimentation, cutting on the brains, making people living vegetables, without the consent. Nobody knows what's going on.

Right now—you say, we're not having any concentration camps.

The jails are filled with nothing but poor. Senator Brooke said the prisons of the United States are filled with eighty percent black, poor, white, Chicano, most of them black. He said that's already a concentration camp.

You say, well, they're there because they committed crime. Oh, is that so? They were hungry, and they wanted some food.

Fifty percent of the black youth today have no jobs. Fifty percent of the black, the Indians have no jobs. Unemployment's rising rapidly. The prime interest is nine point seven today. You know what it was in the Crash of 1929? Ten.

This country has always had to have a war or a depression. I tell you, we're in danger tonight, from a corporate dictatorship. We're in danger from a great fascist state, or a great communist state, and if the church doesn't build a utopian society, build an egalitarian society, we're going to be in trouble.

Four

On a Mission in
Guyana, South America

Peoples Temple voted to establish an agricultural and rural development mission in Guyana, South America, in October 1973. Several months later, a small group of members traveled to Guyana to scout a location for the mission and to establish headquarters in Georgetown, Guyana's capital. They applied to lease twenty-five thousand acres in northwest Guyana, near the border with Venezuela. Working with local villagers, they cleared land in the jungle for farming and construction of the mission's facilities. In 1976 the Guyanese government formally granted Peoples Temple a long-term lease of 3,824 acres for their agricultural project. By that time, construction was underway for a large communal kitchen, a hospital clinic, schoolrooms, cottages, dormitories, a childcare center, and an open-air pavilion.

As the agricultural mission was becoming established in Guyana, Peoples Temple's community outreach activities were in full swing in California. The church hosted events with internationally famous political leaders, participated in spiritual jubilees with the Islamic community, rallied against apartheid, and endorsed the boycott of Florida citrus in response to the anti-gay campaign of citrus spokesperson Anita Bryant. They demonstrated in support of affirmative action, the Black Panthers, and the *Bee* Four, or Fresno Four, who were journalists from the *Sacramento Bee* who were jailed for refusing to name their sources. Peoples Temple sponsored flu inoculation and contributed to social services for seniors, pets, and neighborhoods in San Francisco. Religion in American Life, a national interfaith organization, listed Jones as one of the "100 most outstanding clergymen" of 1975. The *Los Angeles Times* named him "Humanitarian of the Year" in 1976. Later that year, Jim Jones was appointed to a housing commission in San Francisco. In 1977, the National Newspaper Publishers presented their annual Freedom of the Press Award to Peoples Temple.

Peoples Temple members were actively raising funds and promoting their agricultural project in Guyana, which they also called the promised land or the freedom land. Members who planned to live and work on the mission in Guyana were expected to live communally in the United States, and they were encouraged to turn over their assets to the church as a prerequisite for traveling to the agricultural mission. From 1975 to 1978, scores of members deeded homes, automobiles, rental properties, acreage, and inherited property to Peoples Temple with the expectation of a life-care guarantee. Peoples Temple set up a committee to help hundreds of their members to apply for passports, fill out documents required by the Guyanese government, and obtain essential vaccinations.

Behind the scenes of Peoples Temple's public activities, some members were becoming disillusioned and disturbed about the disciplinary practices of the church and about Jim Jones's sexual involvement with members. From 1975 to 1977, a number of active members left the church—some taking their families with them, others leaving relatives behind who remained committed to Peoples Temple. In 1977, a group of these former members organized the Concerned Relatives and Citizens Committee to protest Jones's treatment of members. Property theft, fraud, child custody issues, and living conditions in the Guyana mission, which became known as Jonestown, were at the center of the conflicts between Peoples Temple and the Concerned Relatives. By the spring of 1978, both groups filed lawsuits, sought public support through the media, and appealed to U.S. government officials for protection.

Media coverage of Peoples Temple practices and political activities led the government to investigate the church's financial and social welfare programs. In response to the investigations, Peoples Temple closed many of their businesses, moved their funds from domestic banks to international financial institutions, sold their properties, and facilitated the relocation of hundreds of their members to Guyana.

Jim Jones moved to Guyana in the summer of 1977. While waiting for their opportunity to travel to Jonestown, some members who had been based in Los Angeles and Redwood Valley moved to San Francisco, where Peoples Temple continued to maintain communal housing and hold services and meetings.

"Settin' around Here Free This Morning"
David Betts Jackson
1978

David Betts Jackson, affectionately called Pop Jackson, and his wife, Luvenia, were early settlers of Jonestown. They lived in the small village of Port Kaituma, six miles from the agricultural mission, until housing was built. Pop Jackson was thought to be more than one hundred years old when his personal history was recorded in 1978, but he was actually eighty-six years old.

I'm settin' around here free this morning. Ain't nobody got no pistol on me. Ain't nobody running up behind me, "Pull over there." The white man always wanted to know what you doing—where you been last night. "Put your hands on that car," and they go around putting stuff in your pocket. You better take that stuff out of my pocket.

Everybody that come up that want to do something for a nigger they shot him. They shot Martin Luther for trying to talk for his race. They killed the two Kennedy brothers for trying to talk for the people. Shot him right through the head. And you tell me… ahh, shit. They say, "This is the white man's world." As long as you work with the white man you live. If you didn't, they do you just like Martin Luther, you're shot.

You know one thing. I seen white folks just come right out and just kill niggers. A nigger passed church one Sunday morning on his way home and he was whistling and he got in his car and went 'round that way and cut that nigger off. He got right out of his car—the nigger was whistling a tune, you know—and went right up behind him and shot him through the head. That was in Shreveport, Louisiana. He killed that nigger dead as a hammer. The police come and said, "Who done this?" The man said "me," the policeman said, "You done a good job." You think I wanted to live in a place like that?

I could spend my life sitting here telling you, because I spent my life back there. And all the dirty things, I'm telling you they happened. Now, when it comes to Jonestown, I'm telling you it was the best place what ever was. I had never been to a place like this. It ain't been took up and dried up and you take the best and I take the worst. I want Jonestown to be cared for because it cared for me.

When I came here it was just getting started. I been fooling around the United States for a hundred years and it didn't do a thing for me. The United States is the last place you ought to stop to. You in danger. You should go around that, because if you'll go around, you'll live longer.

I was just laying down last night in my bed, looking up in the roof and I say, "Free at last, free at last." One hundred years under slavery. They used to hire me out and they draw the money in and make you jump in the river. You're gonna drown or you're gonna get killed. So what you gonna do? Last hired and first knocked off. If the white man made two dollars, I made fifty cents.

I had some land back there and they done took it. It had some oil on it. They done took it. My wife had land with an oilfield on it—they done took it. They took it and put us outdoors. No, I ain't going back there. One [hundred] years of slavery is enough for me. You don't know—you really don't know—just how much Jonestown means to me after that.

Memo to U.S. Secretary of State
Deputy Chief of Mission John Blacken
April 19, 1977

Occasionally, American Embassy officials in Guyana would visit Jonestown, one hundred and fifty miles away from the embassy's headquarters in Georgetown. Peoples Temple members who lived in Georgetown often visited the embassy to discuss the progress of the agricultural mission and elicit help in dealing with the Guyanese government.

From: American Embassy Georgetown
To: Secretary of State
Limited Official Use
Subject: 380 Members of Peoples Temple in California Plan to
Immigrate to Guyana

1. Foreign Minister Wills on March 31 gave charge copy of memo of conversation between Vilbert Mingo Minister of Home Affairs and Bishop Jim Jones of Peoples Temple a religious organization located in California, who presently have approximately 40 members of their organization farming outside Port Kaituma in the northwest territory of Guyana.

2. The conversation pertained to a decision on the part of the Peoples Temple to have 380 members of their organization immigrate to Guyana on Sunday, April 3 by two chartered planes. Minister Mingo requested that Peoples

Temple officials postpone the arrival of these 380 prospective immigrants to Thursday, April 7 pending further information about their bonafides. GOG [Government of Guyana] has requested that the list of 380 persons including the number of men, women and children be forwarded to Claude Worrell at the Guyanese Embassy in Washington for his review before permission to enter Guyana can be given.

3. After the meeting took place, James Mentore, Chief of Special Branch, who was present at the meeting, indicated that the delay in the arrival of the 380 persons would give Worrell the opportunity to check their backgrounds with the police in California and then forward this information on to Guyana. At this time date of arrival of group is still undecided pending completion of background checks.

4. The most disturbing aspect that surfaced in the meeting is a statement by Bishop Jones to the Guyanese when he indicated that the 380 prospective immigrants "represent some of the most skilled and progressive elements of his organization and as such are the most vulnerable to state repression on the part of the American authorities."

5. At this meeting the Bishop also exhibited an envelope that he claimed contained a check for $500,000 that he intended to deposit in the Bank of Guyana for use of the intending immigrants to help them settle. He also spoke of his intention to have all or most of the assets of his organization transferred to Guyana.

6. GOG is also concerned about rationale behind Bishop Jones' decision to suddenly bring large numbers of Americans to Guyana. Wills is apprehensive that Jones is carrying out this operation because of possible hostility on the part of his organization toward the USG [United States Government] and publish literature attacking US. GOG is also concerned that the group may have been smuggling foodstuffs into Guyana and Mentore has suggested the need to establish a police outpost in the region.

7. On the other hand Peoples Temple organization currently has a good reputation with GOG as an industrious, hard-working organization who is helping to develop Guyana's interior. In this connection Peoples Temple officials here have close working relationships with the Ministry of National Development. GOG therefore while chary of program, nevertheless has no reason to deny entry if members of the group are eligible in all other respects of Guyanese Law.

Letters from Guyana
Maria Katsaris
c. 1977

Peoples Temple in Guyana communicated with their members in the U.S. by amateur (ham) radio, telephone, and international mail. Members who traveled back and forth between Guyana and the U.S. also carried correspondence and documents. Maria Katsaris wrote these two letters, the first from Jonestown and the second from Georgetown, to one of the people in charge of procuring supplies and shipping them from the U.S. She was one of several people, including Carolyn Layton, who oversaw the finances of Peoples Temple.

The packets she refers to are large envelopes filled with letters written by Jonestown residents to their families and friends in the U.S. Her reference to #3, at the end of her first letter, was her telephone extension at the Peoples Temple church in San Francisco.

Hi Randolph!

Here I am in the middle of the jungle, roughing it on this IBM typewrite typewriter. However, I am having some problems ᵗᵏᵃᵗ As you can see. This thing sticks. Bad. But I think it is the moisture   here, because its always something different that sticks. I'll own up to all the typos, but not to the   wierdo spacing. Anyways, I'm trying to see if leaving it turned on for a while and using it will dry it up. Otherwise you might never have been honored to receive this wonderful letter. There are a few odds and ends needed here. Freezer paper is one. If some could be sent now and then a large amoun amount with a shipment it would be good. Paper is hard to come by. Also, please ask Ruby to go to the Daly City Akron's and see if they have special candles to repel misquitos. Someone said they have them there and she knows something about them, otherwise they would have to be hunted up somewhere else. There are none of those little buggers here in the P.L. but in town its different. The only place those creeps get you is on your feet! Pleaes ask the procurement people to try and get some women's bras. All sizes but mainly 34's and 36's ᶻᵃˢᵐᵘᵗᶜʰⁱⁿᵍ. I alxmost forgot something. You know the seeds that were bought, right? Well, I [hate] to break this to you but they never got here with Leona's group. I think they were packed in a brown suitcase by Debbie with a bunch of other odds and ends like Terry's Omega watch. Can you get someone to try and track that thing down. In all the confusion in L.A., it may not have even gotten loaded in the van. And last of all next time someone comes stick in a couple of 6 volt adapters for taperecorders

All business aside, you would not believe this place. Everytime I come I can't get over it. Jonestown is huge! Just when you think that you can't be ~~impress~~ anymore impressed with all the house~~s~~s, dorms, classrooms, playground, crops, you go down to the piggery, cassava mill, and chicken houses, and you can't believe all that has ~~done~~ been done. Anyways, Randolph, I'm just trying [to] prepare you for the fact that I might not come back. I really don't want to and I don't want to blow my big chance, if you ~~a~~ know what I mean! That's the way it goes! Take care of the packets for me, and you can always call #3 and pretend that youre talking (bugging) me. O.K. Say hi to all the people in your department and give them greetings from J.T. with Fathers love   maria

To: Jim Randolph   *Let me know what I can do from this end while I'm here.*
From: Maria
Re: More Stuff

- PLEASE!!! Make sure that everyone who comes has the phone number to the house here.
- People should bring their resumes and college transcripts with them so they can get a job in Georgetown. Maybe people should start sending away for that stuff so it is in their files and ready to go. But I would only worry about those we know who have college educations and employable skills. Not someone who was in the class of 1899.
- It would be helpful if things like moth balls, needles, thread, buttons, zippers, diapers, toilet paper, powdered Isomil or Soylac, hangers, office supplies, could be stashed in each person's bags. And absolutely, each person should carry their own bedding in their own stuff.
- last time I asked you about x looking into misquito ~~repledn~~ repellant candles. I saw one that is down here and all they are are regularx parafin candles with citronella oil added. Maybe some of the people in the old candle making crew could just make them.
- we need a iron here in town and some rubberbands. Also, tube socks and umbrellas if people have them, just a few.
- we have a problem in the interior because of shortage of socks. The people who have been here for three years have worn out all their stuff. So extra

socks should be sent. Also, it should be made clear to ~~everybody~~ people coming, just because they have 12 pair of socks, t shirts, etc., does not mean all 12 [are] all theirs to keep. Things like that will be distributed. Also, clothes should be left unmarked until they get to JT.

- will you have someone check into the price of pull over rubber boots? The kind for the interior. But don't get them yet. We may be able to get them for a low price, but just want to double check.
- why aren't people using duffle bags instead of all these trunks??? If there is a reason please tell me. It seems that ~~clothin~~ clothing can be packed into duffle bags and other supplies in trunks. It didn't make too much sense to me to see all these trunks, even for the babies. Couldn't we use the duffle bags Ruby's crew makes. You can even buy large, used army surplus duffle bags on mission street for $2.99 which is still cheaper than the trunks.

Well, thats all I can come up ~~with~~ with for now. I know you love me. I miss all you guys, but not where you are! Just feel guilty not being ~~hx~~ there to help you with all that is going on. mk

"Jim's Commentary about Himself"
Jim Jones
1977–1978

Jim Jones moved to Jonestown in the summer of 1977. As part of their efforts to document his biography and the history of Peoples Temple, members recorded his remarks on his religious and political background.

William Farr, mentioned here, was a *Los Angeles Times* reporter who had been jailed for refusing to name sources while he was covering the Charles Manson trials in the early 1970s. Peoples Temple had demonstrated and written letters on his behalf as they would several years later for the "Fresno four."

I shall call myself a Marxist, because certainly no one taught me my brand of Marxism. I read. I listened. I went back to the university and I met another couple of communists. I guess I sought them out. Old time pro-Soviet Communists. They were so gracious. They received me in their home. A father and the son. The mother had died. Humble home outside of Bloomington, Indiana, where I went to university… Those were the people I sought for inspiration.

Peoples Temple youth in Redwood
Valley. MSP 3800

Peoples Temple youth in the church's
community gardens in Redwood Valley.
MSP 3800

Peoples Temple members relaxing. Community meals were an integral part of Peoples Temple weekend services and important stops on their frequent bus trips. MSP 3800

Senior member at homemade pie and cake table. Peoples Temple members ran a concession stand and a gift shop where they sold anointed cloths, oils, and photographs of Jim Jones and his family in Redwood Valley. MSP 3800

Seniors gathered in the community room of the Redwood Valley
church to make pillows for a church fundraiser. MSP 3800

Peoples Temple church service in Los Angeles. MSP 3800

Children of Peoples Temple members on the steps of the
Los Angeles Temple. Jim Jones at the top of the steps.
MSP 3800

Peoples Temple church in Los Angeles. 1972. MSP 3800

Seniors at a Peoples Temple service in San Francisco. MSP 3800

Members dancing after a church service. Peoples Temple sponsored large adult and youth choirs, bands, and dance groups. MSP 3800

Members in the Peoples Temple woodshop in San Francisco.
MSP 3800

Then I developed a definite concept with the problems of the world, the misery of the world, two out of three babies going to bed hungry—as late as the Nixon years, when President Nixon pronounced that that was the case. I don't remember the statistics of that time, but they certainly must have been hard, indeed. It seemed gross to me that one human being would have so much more than another. I couldn't come to terms with capitalism in any way. I wanted to. I wanted to retreat from this gnawing sense of conscience that pushed me forward.

Then I decided, *where* can I demonstrate my Marxism? I demonstrated it in many places, and almost got into trouble in classrooms. An agent checked on me because of my activities that took me to a Paul Robeson event. I went through considerable harassments that are unpleasant and painful. My mother was questioned by the FBI for several hours, brought out, and interrogated in front of an open area where all of her fellow workers at the factory would see her. And she was a shop stewardess. And, I recall, thereafter was relieved because of being questioned about my activities. She took the Fifth Amendment. In those days, you did not do that. That was tantamount to admission of being a communist. And my poor mom knew nothing at all of politics. She was as apolitical as she could be. She believed in her son, which certainly has helped. Perhaps to some degree it hurt, but I would prefer the chances of the kind of belief that she had. She was a little indulgent of me at times, certainly from her limited means, but solid as the rock of Gibraltar. She endured, not knowing even what I was up to as they didn't even tell her—that it was merely because I had been to an event where Paul Robeson sang and participated in Chicago. She didn't know what I had done, but she defended me. She said I refuse to testify on the grounds it might tend to incriminate me or my son...

So on down the road, I became even more alienated by that event. I decided, *how* can I demonstrate my Marxism? The thought was "infiltrate the church." I consciously made a decision to look into that prospect... I had had my religious heritage in Pentecostalism—deep-rooted emotions in the Christian tradition— and a deep love, which I share to this day, for the practical teachings of Jesus Christ. It had always been a sort of dual concept—a doubter, and yet, a believer. Certainly I had great questions about anthropomorphic beings and a loving order to the universe, but Jesus Christ, to use the kids' phrase, greatly turned me on. And I tried very hard through my years in the church—wherever someone else might look upon my role, however they would look upon it, they would see a great deal of sensitivity to the Christian teachings. Not only my brand of Marxism, but in

[the] Pentecostal tradition. I saw that when the early believers came together, they sold their possessions and had all things common. I tried very hard to live up to that concept throughout my years.

In the early years, I'd approached Christendom from a communal standpoint, with only intermittent mention of my Marxist views. However, in later years, there wasn't a person that attended any of my meetings that did not hear me say, at some time, that I was a communist. And that is what is very strange, that all these years, I have survived without being exposed.

The news media were concerned that we were overreacting to coverage, as if only it was that that concerned me—that my exposure as a communist would affect the lives and well-being of my most precious family, and dearest associates—and in fact, all of my church that had become an extended family. I was fearful of nothing else. There was nothing else in my life that I was afraid of being revealed. But I think the media made a grave mistake in thinking that we, during the Nixon years, assisted—at least I got the impression from some that they have thought that—that we assisted people like Farr because we were trying to get on the good side of the press. I really couldn't think you could get on the good side of the press, because being a communist, I believed that the press—the myth of the adversary press—to me was very, very real. But whatever adversary role it played, it looked like it was played out in the Nixon years. So I took my stance. And then again, when I saw the Fresno situation, it reminded me all too well of that era, where newsmen were going to jail for their sources about corruption at a higher level. By the same token, people who are anonymous sources could be devastating to little people who are unable to protect themselves. The right of confidentiality of sources to reveal high-level corruption was very important to me.

One of the reasons I'm telling my story is because I certainly don't feel any inclination as a writer. I have still great apprehension that the press—with the exception of some in the black and some of the communist and socialist press—have the feeling that it would not give me a fair story. And that's all I want—a fair story. Then again, I really don't, at this point, give a damn as to whether I have personal fairness—but as I am affected, so are all of my people. I have developed, through the years, a high sensitivity to all the members of my church. They are, as to me, an extended family. I don't want to hurt them. I want to try to give them some relief of suffering. Perhaps this writing will help that. I feel no idea that writing is that significant. Great writers have written and their words have been forgotten too soon with their departure, or if even remembered at any time, whether they were alive or dead. So, my main reason for writing is to help protect my people. I really have a strong desire to die at the time of this writing. I have been imprisoned in my mind for many, many years—constantly trying to conceal a lifestyle alien to the American society that would have caused great pain for my devoted and precious wife and those who followed on in my footsteps to become socialist or communist. Some I don't think understood the difference, but everyone in our parish certainly subscribes to some form of socialism.

I am not about to make any kind of great conversion speech. I would not want to do anything but give the absolute honesty of my soul. I told you of the duality in my mind. A part of me emotionally is caught up with the Christian tradition. I'm more comfortable in the warmth of a Pentecostal setting. And that's why I sought that kind of a lifestyle, because it was in that setting—of freedom of emotion—that I felt my first acceptance. I found that same kind of spirit in the communist rallies that I attended. No matter what disillusionment I may have—I have come to the point that I'm a communalist. I sought haven in a socialist country. I theoretically feel that communism in unattainable in the terms of man's present evolution in a nuclear technology. But I do believe that a communal lifestyle offers much to people, and it certainly is greatly accepted in the republic in which we lived in at the time of this writing, where we have received gracious acceptance. It's not easy forging out a new community in the midst of a jungle, and we have done that.

Letter to Jim Jones
Marceline Jones
August 15, 1977

Marceline Jones often traveled between Guyana and the U.S. In the wake of allegations published in the summer of 1977 in the California magazine *New West* and the *San Francisco Examiner*, she wrote to Jim Jones about changing the disciplinary practices of the community in Jonestown. Peoples Temple members often used code names in their correspondence and in ham radio transmissions to and from Jonestown; hence she signs this letter under the name Irene.

Dearest Jim,

We are getting much publicity about corporal punishment being used. Certainly it is grossly exaggerated. However, while you are there—you must, I think, impress upon those in charge that they must be careful of the forms of discipline and isolation used. Certainly—peer pressure is best. The hard hat and no speaking to the offender is a good example. Now that you have young people there who are not discipline problems—you can use the peer pressure. Before—it was near impossible because the only peer pressure there was from young people who had been totally destroyed by this system and had some bizarre behavior patterns...

Love all of you so much,

Irene [Marceline]

"Who are the People of Jonestown?"
Dick Tropp
c. 1978

After Dick Tropp moved to Jonestown in September 1997, he continued writing for Peoples Temple. He edited members' submissions for a book on conspiracies against Jim Jones and Peoples Temple and drafted articles for international publications and pamphlets for the Guyanese public about the agricultural project.

The excerpt below is from a piece that he originally conceived as a "dramatic reading for four to five voices."

We are America's offspring, many the children and grandchildren of a heritage of slavery and forced labor, painful realities quite opposite of the ideals of freedom, justice, concern for the individual that American society supposedly fosters.

Factory workers, wage-slaves, people who toiled in the "pastures of plenty" for starvation pay and perpetual misery; domestics, migrants, people who rode the rails seeking for jobs, who picked for food scraps among the refuse of your cities, among the wastes of people who never saw us, never cared. White, black, red and brown, haggard children of the unemployed in every city, children of subsistence farmers in the Midwest and South, children of the depression that never really ended, labor organizers, veterans of hunger marches, protests, union struggles, relief lines. We are America's "niggers..." We are people who saw our brothers and husbands lynched and castrated, who walked the streets in fear, who worried endlessly about children who never came home.

We, too, are those children, who searched the endless mean streets, the rotted-out insides of decayed cities, unable to find the America we saw on television...

We are the people who never fit into the slots. From whatever place we came, we had this in common: we sensed something was wrong, terribly wrong. There was a plague raging among us, and it had gotten into us, making us sick in a hundred ways. All the appearances of plenty, the supermarkets of consumer junk, the false symbols of affluence, the abundance that was really only one man's way of stealing from a million, only imperfectly covered up a terrible wound, a great festering ulcer that dug into the guts of our society, and into our lives.

But is was often a subtle soul sickness; with it came the dull weight of a feeling that nothing was of any use, that *we* weren't of any use; we were trapped in a prison without walls, even when we had thought we made it out, we discovered that we were still caught, our lives without a center; even the old institutions of family and church where we sought refuge were crumbling, and brought no relief, only an intensification, a reminder of the pain, a reminder that we were nowhere, in a wasteland of broken promises…

From that slow death of the spirit, that nameless emptiness that penetrated through whatever we might manage to patch together to ward it off, many of us sought in desperation for a refuge.

We found each other. Our experiences, our backgrounds, were what had kept us apart, but our longing and sickness brought us together, in a terrible realization that we were all victims. And it took one great honest human being who could remind us of that deeply concealed truth, who could articulate that ache of the spirit. Through his compassion, wisdom and ability to penetrate to those lower depths, to touch us at the heart of our heart's ache, our pent-up longings and deferred dreams, and to confront us at the convergence of the thousand unanswered questions, and the endless, impossible contradictions of our lives—he has brought us together—to heal the wounds by making us realize that we were hurting in common and hurting each other and that we need to do something about it, that we were human, and all the same flesh and blood and mind and spirit; that we needed each other, not the cheap props and cosmetics of advertising and politics, the celluloid and televised visions and excuses of what we could never be.

We are the people of Jonestown. Former church ministers, attorneys, nobodies, aimless college students, secretaries, pushers, prostitutes, labor organizers, social workers, Peace Corps veterans; people who searched and found, were lost, got sidetracked, stuck; jailbirds, salesmen, machinists, designers, card sharks, professors, ditch-diggers, railroaders, artists, jet pilots; accountants, scientists, domestics, draftsmen and actors; high school sports champions, exotic dancers, half-educated, miseducated, uneducated; health-food nuts and junk food addicts.…

part of the vast underclass that looks at "progress" over a great unbridgeable chasm, through wires and glass and iron that won't yield, like a child trying to find the gleaming, fleeting jet plane in a distant sky filled with its noise and exhaust.

We come from everywhere, from every corner of the nation, from every walk of life. But you won't find among us a single oil executive, diplomat, politician, judge, board chairman, casino owner, landlord, chain store magnate, or bank president. Or anybody "who had it made." We didn't "have it made." Even if we did in the eyes of the world, we knew something was wrong.

And now today, we have shaken the dust and filth of America's cities of despair from our tired feet.

Reverend Jim Jones worked for 25 years in the United States, fought racists, faced assassination attempts, struggled against hordes of detractors, organized, talked endlessly, traveled millions of miles and spoke to millions of persons in thousands of places, building, sacrificing all personal comforts, putting his life at the service of others, spending endless nights helping people who often would abuse and turn against him, taking on the toughest situation, and riding them through, not giving up.

Now, having seen the handwriting on the wall, having seen that his work would never really succeed as he wanted it to in an environment that was inhospitable and increasingly hostile, he began this community.

We have come here, the people of Jonestown, and we have come to build. We have our remorse, our bitterness, our scars. They will never go away. But Jim Jones has always believed in lighting candles rather than cursing the darkness. And we are determined to let our light shine.

from "Instructions from JJ"
March 17–May 25, 1978

In Jonestown, Peoples Temple held community meetings, called Peoples Rallies, in the open-air pavilion. Sometimes these meetings were recorded on audiotape. Often, members took notes and typed them up for the community bulletin boards.

The "Instructions" were a cumulative list of rules that covered many aspects of daily life and behavior in Jonestown. The "New Brigade" was a work group that people were assigned to for infractions against the community rules. Item

33 on the list refers to the common practice of members changing their names to reflect personal preferences and their admiration for their political heroes. Item 42 refers to six-year-old John Stoen, who was at the center of a custody battle between his parents and Jim Jones.

The "Instructions" and the "Follow-Up Notes" also include very specific rules governing how Jonestown residents were to interact with guests. From 1976 to 1978, guests that visited Jonestown included California Lieutenant Governor Mervyn Dymally, officials of the American Embassy and the Guyanese government, members of the Guyanese public, representatives of the USSR, attorneys and filmmakers from the U.S., and relatives of Peoples Temple members. Annie Moore and Carolyn (Moore) Layton's parents visited the agricultural project in May 1978. Marceline Jones's parents were in Jonestown in late October and early November 1978.

INSTRUCTIONS FROM JJ
Since: March 17, 1978
1. People on New Brigade one, two and three times can get off at any time with good work attitude. Put people on the fifth time will stay 10 weeks,
2. Anyone with any anarchist will be suspect.
3. People in trouble will be on the New Brigade permanently if they associate with one another and they will be living under a military type situation

3-25
4. Any Socialism teacher that allows a student to go to the bathroom will go on the New Brigade.
5. If someone makes fun of others, bypass all committees and take them straight to the New Brigade.
6. Don't give anyone anything—turn it back into Central Supply.
7. Don't make announcements on the speakers when guests are here unless it's cleared by JJ personally.
8. Socialism classes: Make them smaller in size, take roll and give work assignments.
9. All bedwetters are to be moved to D-l immediately. They will be awakened by security. Move everyone else out to the cottages so that they can have relief from the tensions there. We will define psychological bedwetters from those with physical problems.

10. Don't you dare say "Write me up" or you will automatically go on the Red Brigade.

11. Security for Crews: Each time you come in, turn in your arms so they can be used. They will be reassigned each morning.

12. Until further notice someone in your department will be bearing arms. Wherever you are, someone will be able to protect you....

13. JJ is going to destroy thievery or the thieves.

14. Have patience with people who have speech problems.

15. When you are black and oppressed, it's treason to not want to think.

16. I can't leave this place... too much security will be gone. You can't trust people who don't bother to know what goes on in the news.

17. No one is going to town except entertainers.

3-27

18. When are the benches with backs going to be finished?

19. Tape recorders are to be checked in and recorded. No mikes are to be kept on them.

4-4

20. Remember people who are on the New Brigade one day at a time... if you give any shit, you will be on for a long time.

21. Don't you dare say, "Write me up." It's anarchy. If you say it you are in trouble.

4-20

22. Don't go out of our local area. We have an infiltrator that will be waiting to get out... as soon as pressures mount.

23. Pick up all possible cats in Georgetown. The boat is not to leave without cats...

5-4

33. Get a name and stick with it so that we can know what it is...

42. Lee Ingram, remind children to not talk amongst themselves or to John. (About kidnapping, etc.)...

50. People with ringworm and sores are to take a shower before treatment.

51. People who sleep in service go automatically to the New Brigade.

52. Don't walk around in nightclothes.

53. JJ wants to see more people reading.

54. News: JJ will accept what is being read from books that show principle.

55. Classes will really have to work on teaching.

56. People need to spend time in the library to get information. The tape can be stopped.

57. Everyone should go over the news in discussion groups. Every cottage.

58. All of us have to look at education. You can whisper in someone's ear the meaning of words. Names are difficult.

59. Order the material needed for visual films so maps can be shown.

60. Professor Roller will have an additional class at 1 P.M. She is to also have night classes.

61. I want them to get that boat.

62. JJ wants a progress report. He doesn't trust hospitals. (Baby in G.T.)…

75. Confer: don't make independent decisions.

76. Write relatives and ask for a watch. Get something out of them. Be creative…

83. We have to get rid of maggots. I hate the word "research", when will we find the solution?

84. The kitchen didn't know that the wheat came in and JJ said it had better not happen again.

85. Tell no one the formula for making soap…

101. We have to get some enthusiasm in what we believe.

102. When you have a Soviet map up, you have to have a map of the U.S.

103. You have to get approval if leaving the kitchen area to eat. If not, you are in trouble.

104. Someone will have to start and stop the tape. Train some people. (News.)

105. Analysts, we have to educate. Meet with the crews.

106. We have to see that the news gets to Georgetown. Send a secret memo and then destroy it.

107. Dishes caught laying around and your ass should be on the New Brigade.

108. We can't afford to give medications away. Give medications only in case of a baby dying.

109. Get free medication… the economy is in bad shape. This will have to be cleared on a one to one basis. JJ would never deny medication for kidney infection.

110. Refer [patients] to Georgetown, we will take them on our boat.

111. Break heaven and earth to get medicine tomorrow. (5-21-78)

112. Iron deficiency is dangerous.

113. Recommend diets to the people, Doctor.

114. Alice Ingram is to start in Central Supply immediately (5-21-78).

115. Don't you ever let the power go out here. It could be in the middle of a medical emergency...

from "Follow-up Notes from Peoples Rally"
August 8, 1978

10)　If they ask what happens if you don't follow the rules? Say that it is a community problem and is handled in our town forum—we have a total democracy: everybody has a voice. We deny them few privileges for few days.

11)　DO NOT USE THE WORD FAMILY—because of the Mooney family, and the Manson family, it has a poor connotation to most U.S. people—the capitalists have done this to weaken the family structure...

14)　If asked why you came here? Because I wanted to... I didn't like the racism. I don't have anything against the United States—my family soon will be coming here. However, we didn't visit that much when we were there, so am not really lonely for them. I just love it here too much to go back...

15)　If asked what kind of work you do...CAUTION IF A SENIOR...say I keep up my yard...work in my garden...sew a little. Seniors aren't required to work, but I like to do some things. We have planned exercise and recreation time—we have plenty to do—or we can just relax when we want to.

16)　What do you do with your money? What do you mean? I have my money—but you don't have to pay here. How much do I have?—REALLY!!! that's my own affair. Really, money doesn't mean much here because you don't need money. I can travel where I want to...I go into Georgetown occasionally and other towns on the coast...

21)　Church?—No, we don't "have" church here. We have town forum every week once, but never more than twice in a week. They don't like you to go if you feel bad—we have nurses that check you and watch over any who aren't well.

22)　We have a lovely warehouse. I get all that I want right there. We call it Central Supply. And my loved ones stateside occasionally send me something. Everyone here gets the same treatment. If you don't have relatives that provide you with things, you can get it from central supply or they will order it for you if it is not on the shelf. All needs are met...

24)　DO NOT SAY WE CAME OVER HERE TO AVOID CONCENTRATION

CAMPS...MAKE *"NO"* REFERENCE TO CONCENTRATION CAMPS AT ALL!!!...

28)   Do not refer to Guyana as the "promised" land—or freedomland. Say, if asked why you came here and did anyone make you....Say, "I made up my own mind...I had heard about it from people who had been over there and returned to the States. It was far more than they had described it to be...

75)   Give your original name when guest is here—do not use your socialist names such as Lenin, Che Guevara, etc....

Self-Analyses and Self-Evaluations
1977–1978

Jim Jones often asked Jonestown residents to write short papers based on what they learned in the classes on history, Russian language, and current events that Peoples Temple offered in Jonestown. He also asked them to write self-analyses and self-evaluations focused on their feelings about his responsibilities, living in Jonestown, their commitment to socialism, sex, and other personal topics. Members would also write summaries of other members' verbal responses to questions posed in public meetings and in smaller meetings.

Hyacinth Thrash and *Zipporah Edwards*, who wrote the following letter, moved to Jonestown in July 1977. They lived in a small cottage with two other women. They decorated it with rugs they hooked themselves and with chairs Pop Jackson made for them in the Jonestown woodshop. Hyacinth Thrash spent much of her time in the cottage. Her sister Zip attended classes on the history of socialism and worked at various times in the radio room, in central supply, where they stored clothing and other personal items, and in the sewing room with other seniors who made toys that Peoples Temple sold to Guyanese stores.

Dear Dad,

I was outside the other night and I looked up at the stars, I never saw such beautiful sight in my life. They all twinkling as though they were saying to me welcome, I am glad you are free from that capitalist society. It is so lovely here in this country. I look back in my life and just think I never dreamed that I would ever be doing the thing I am doing now, working to help liberate all the oppressed people of the world. And I am so grateful to you for making it possible because without you I never would have known what it was all about. It gives one such a good feeling to know that you are doing something for betterment of down-trodden people. And I thank you for giving me a chance to learn and gain knowledge of what's going on in the world and that I can become a true communist. I am going to study harder than ever to learn more. I thank you for all these years I have known you because I know that it was not by chance that I turned on my TV that Sunday morning and you were there. I never will forget the feeling that came over me when I heard you speak. I knew at once that I had found what I had been looking for. And I made my pledge that as long as I lived I never would leave. So I thank you dad for all you have done for everyone. And letting me know who you are. I have always wish I could have walked with the Christ but you proved to be much greater than the one I thought about. And I thank you for allowing me the privilege of walking with you. I thank you for everything. I think on you everyday, and I am blessed to be here. Zipporah Edwards

Dad I wrote this letter about two weeks ago. And it got missed place and the other day Hyacinth found it but never looked to see what it was and threw it in the wastebasket. I went out and emptied it but after some time I looked on my shelf among my clothes and there this letter was. I never thought I would ever see it again. Thank you Dad because I could not have thought of the same words to say again because I am always moved upon to write you. Some time I have gone to bed and all of a sudden I am moved to write about the things that's on my heart. I get right up and do so. Thanks so much.

■ *Harriet S. Tropp* studied law in San Francisco. She moved to Jonestown in August 1977 and became a member of the administrative triumvirate, along with Carolyn Layton and Johnny Moss Brown, who oversaw the management of farming, daily life, and building in Jonestown.

From: Harriet S. Tropp
To: Jim
Re: "Hostilities and the Most Irksome Subject of Sex"
   Hostilities, many of these are petty, but petty or not, they are what piss me off.
   1. I get hostile at having to write notes like this. I know that as the leader of this organization, you need this input etc. but nevertheless I still (quite unreasonably) consider it a gross invasion of my privacy. I figure as long as I'm not

acting out then I should be allowed the dignity of keeping my thoughts, especially on sex, to myself. Considering how completely unattractive I am, having to tell you about sexual attractions etc. is extremely humiliating. I know that humiliation can make a person stronger, but I do resent it—and I recognize that resentment reflects my own concern about my image. (If I didn't care about my image, it wouldn't bother me).

2. I get irritated when you give instructions and I can't keep up. I know that you can't help it—memory and thought processes etc. don't time themselves to suit my writing ability—but it's frustrating. Especially when you go over and over something you've already given instructions on. This is totally unreasonable on my part—I do recognize that—since often you will change or add things etc. but it's one of those things that I get irrationally irritated at. I hope you won't stop giving instructions to me just because I said this.

3. I go up a wall with all the announcements, readings etc over the loud speaker. It is irritating as hell. I know that people have to hear you a certain amount of the time, otherwise they act out, but it can be maddening. I have entertained the thought that you were deliberately using a known psychological technique of interrupting people's thought processes with specific information, so as to keep them in a kind of disjointed state—a state that makes them both more receptive to information fed to them, and less able to do concentrated (and often treasonous) things. Of course, this could also be counterproductive, since interruptions do interfere with the ability to do long stretches of efficient work. Whatever your reasons, it is driving me nuts.

4. I get hostile at you when I think you are treating me in what I consider a "dependent" fashion, although that is not the right word, perhaps. For example, I cannot stand when you call me "daughter" and I am glad you don't do it often. I consider my ties to you and this organization to be deeper, and of a much different quality than any stupid "blood-tie" or psuedo "blood-tie." You are not my "dad" and I do not think of you as such. I think of us as comrades—you, of course of a much greater character, sensitivity, and commitment than I, but comrades nevertheless...

Sex

Yes, I'd like to fuck you—if it were possible to divorce ourselves from time and space, if it were just a question of hopping into bed and fucking—sure. I don't think you are "handsome" in any stupid, superficial way—you are 47 and fat. But I do feel a closeness to you, based on working with you etc. etc. that one half wishes could be translated into a physical thing. You know, a nice fuck between friends. I don't have romantic illusions.

They say the greatest orgasm is death, so I hope we will have the great pleasure of dying together.

■ *Christine Miller* was a member of Peoples Temple from Los Angeles. She moved to Guyana in January 1978. She later proposed that she return to the U.S. to work and send money to support Peoples Temple in Jonestown.

I am grateful for the experience that I have had since coming to Jonestown. I am not too happy now, though, as you may know, maybe because I do not have the peace that I had expected. Maybe I am thinking about myself too much. I should be more concerned about others.

I am concerned about your health as the Leader, about the future of the children. I am interested in learning and knowledge, but it seems we are so pushed, trying to work every day and produce, and trying to get the news off [chalk] boards, when there is so little paper, no time to study.

I am used to traveling often, and I can't do that here, and this bothers me. I'm used to doing what I want to do, when I want to do it. It seems that I'm in a cage like a bird. I haven't gotten adjusted. I don't think that I have made much of a contribution toward the cause by coming here. I feel that I am a liability rather than an asset. This bothers me. I look at myself and wonder why I am living. To me I am merely existing. I don't see that I am accomplishing anything. Sometimes I feel like crying, and sometimes I do, but who is it that don't weep sometime.

I am a tired person, very very tired. I have worked hard all my born days. Started in the fields when I was too small to pull a cotton sack, and left motherless at a very early age. I worked hard, pulled up by my own bootstraps. No one helped me. Now that I'm older & my pace is slower, I don't like to be pushed.

I have no sexual ambitions. I have overcome that thank goodness.

I am very happy you stopped the fighting among ourselves and the hostility among ourselves on the floor. I am totally against that. More love should be shown among ourselves. But it's hard to show it here for it seems when you do you get your ass kicked. Some enjoy cursing, beating and knocking others around. I am against this.

I want to live the rest of my days quietly and peaceful, this is all I ask for. Please let me do this.

"Peoples Temple Show: A Success!"
Guyana Chronicle
April 14, 1978

As part of their outreach activities in Guyana, Peoples Temple participated in cultural events in Georgetown, the capital city. Members of the band and other performers from Jonestown were carefully screened by Jim Jones and other leaders for each trip away from Jonestown. This review is from a Georgetown paper.

The Peoples Temple Agricultural Project presented its cultural variety show entitled "A Cooperative Feeling" last week at the National Cultural Center with a style never before seen in Guyana, which literally prompted the audience to shout for more, following some of the performances. The theme of Cooperation was carried throughout the program, which consisted of over 20 different presentations, including Guyana's own Atlantic Symphony Orchestra and the Yoruba Singers. Although the program ran past midnight few people could be seen leaving....

Most of the show's song and dance numbers were accompanied by a brass band, "Jonestown Express," which one experienced stage crewman said was the best band he had heard in the Caribbean. He noted the hard work put in by the band, which often rehearsed from morning till midnight during the week preceding the show.

The presentation of donations raised by the Peoples Temple was made to various local charities, including the National Relief Committee, the Maha Saba Temple (a home for orphans), Bellfield Home for the Aged and the Guyana Council of Churches (of which Peoples Temple is a member)....

The program was not without its light moments both in song and dances, as well as in comedy skits. One act was a man with red wavy hair, dressed in a glittering jump suit, high heeled boots and dark glasses—a new rock and roll singing sensation. Young girls went screaming onto the stage hysterically, trying to get a memento of his attire. All that was left when they finished with him was a fat old man in polka dot undershorts and with a bald head. They even took his false teeth. The audience roared and few could miss the statement on how some singing stars are nothing more than packaged commodities.

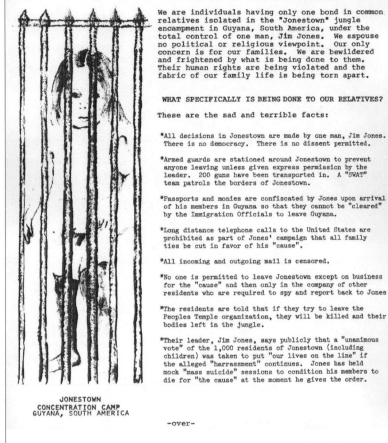

THIS NIGHTMARE IS TAKING PLACE RIGHT NOW

WILL YOU HELP US FREE OUR FAMILIES?

WHO ARE THE "CONCERNED RELATIVES"?

We are individuals having only one bond in common relatives isolated in the "Jonestown" jungle encampment in Guyana, South America, under the total control of one man, Jim Jones. We espouse no political or religious viewpoint. Our only concern is for our families. We are bewildered and frightened by what is being done to them. Their human rights are being violated and the fabric of our family life is being torn apart.

WHAT SPECIFICALLY IS BEING DONE TO OUR RELATIVES?

These are the sad and terrible facts:

*All decisions in Jonestown are made by one man, Jim Jones. There is no democracy. There is no dissent permitted.

*Armed guards are stationed around Jonestown to prevent anyone leaving unless given express permission by the leader. 200 guns have been transported in. A "SWAT" team patrols the borders of Jonestown.

*Passports and monies are confiscated by Jones upon arrival of his members in Guyana so that they cannot be "cleared" by the Immigration Officials to leave Guyana.

*Long distance telephone calls to the United States are prohibited as part of Jones' campaign that all family ties be cut in favor of his "cause".

*All incoming and outgoing mail is censored.

*No one is permitted to leave Jonestown except on business for the "cause" and then only in the company of other residents who are required to spy and report back to Jones

*The residents are told that if they try to leave the Peoples Temple organization, they will be killed and their bodies left in the jungle.

*Their leader, Jim Jones, says publicly that a "unanimous vote" of the 1,000 residents of Jonestown (including children) was taken to put "our lives on the line" if the alleged "harrassment" continues. Jones has held mock "mass suicide" sessions to condition his members to die for "the cause" at the moment he gives the order.

**JONESTOWN
CONCENTRATION CAMP
GUYANA, SOUTH AMERICA**

-over-

In May 1978, members of the Concerned Relatives and Citizens Committee filed lawsuits against Jim Jones and Peoples Temple and circulated a petition and affidavits from former Jonestown residents to public officials in the U.S. and in Guyana. They distributed this flyer outlining their observations and perceptions of the living conditions in Jonestown.

In 1979, the U.S. State Department reported that a total of thirty-five guns had been found in Jonestown and among Peoples Temple members in Guyana.

Following is the text of the two-page flyer.

This Nightmare is Taking Place Right Now
WILL YOU HELP US FREE OUR FAMILIES?
WHO ARE THE "CONCERNED RELATIVES"?

We are individuals having only one bond in common; relatives isolated in the "Jones town" jungle encampment in Guyana, South America, under the total control of one man, Jim Jones. We espouse no political or religious viewpoint. Our only concern is for our families. We are bewildered and frightened by what is being done to them. Their human rights are being violated and the fabric of our family life is being torn apart.

WHAT SPECIFICALLY IS BEING DONE TO OUR RELATIVES?

These are the sad and terrible facts:

*All decisions in Jonestown are made by one man, Jim Jones. There is no democracy. There is no dissent permitted.

*Armed guards are stationed around Jonestown to prevent anyone leaving unless given express permission by the leader. 200 guns have been transported in. A "SWAT" team patrols the borders of Jonestown.

*Passports and monies are confiscated by Jones upon arrival of his members in Guyana so that they cannot be "cleared" by the Immigration Officials to leave Guyana.

*Long distance telephone calls to the United States are prohibited as part of Jones' campaign that all family ties be cut in favor of his "cause".

*All incoming and outgoing mail is censored.

*No one is permitted to leave Jonestown except on business for the "cause" and then only in the company of other residents who are required to spy and report back to Jones.

*The residents are told that if they try to leave the Peoples Temple organization, they will be killed and their bodies left in the jungle.

*Their leader, Jim Jones, says publicly that a "unanimous vote" of the 1,000 residents of Jonestown (including children) was taken to put "our lives on the line" if the alleged "harrassment" continues. Jones has held mock "mass suicide" sessions to condition his members to die for "the cause" at the moment he gives the order.

WHY ARE WE ASKING YOU AS A "CONCERNED CITIZEN" TO HELP?

Because we are desperate and don't know what else to do. Neither the Guyana government nor the United States government thus far has been willing to intervene. Jones simply ignores court orders.

We want our loved ones to be allowed to live in freedom. There appears to be only one way to achieve this—to publicize the truth and to pressure the Prime Minister of Guyana both directly and through the U.S. State Department. We sent a petition on May 10, 1978, to Prime Minister Burnham requesting him to:

1. Order a governmental investigation of Jonestown with inspectors placed there around the clock.

2. Order Jones to stop violating the human and legal rights of our relatives. Specifically, to order Jones to:

   a. Remove all guards preventing people from leaving Jonestown;

   b. Return passports and money;

   c. Permit our relatives to mix with local Guyanese as individuals;

   d. Stop censoring mail;

   e. Permit our relatives to return home for a one-week visit at our expense, return fare guaranteed, to show they are not being held against their will;

   f. Abide by the lawful orders of the courts in the U.S.

3. Expel Jones from Guyana if he refuses to abide by these orders.

WHAT CAN YOU DO TO HELP US?

Three Things:

*Pray for the safe return of our loved ones soon, even if only for a one-week home visit at our expense, return fare being guaranteed, so we can know they have free will to choose.

*Write to the two officials with power to force Jones to respect human and legal rights:

> Honorable Forbes Burnham
> Prime Minister of the Cooperative Republic of Guyana
> Public Buildings
> Georgetown, Guyana, South America
> and
> Honorable Cyrus Vance
> Secretary of State of the United States
> 2201 "C" Street N.W.
> Washington, D.C. 20520

* Give as you feel led to help defray expenses, which are considerable. Send your check to:

CONCERNED RELATIVES AND CITIZENS
120 Montgomery Street, Suite 1700
San Francisco, California 94104

(An application for tax-exempt status will soon be filed with I.R.S. Our attorneys say "Concerned Relatives and Citizens" meets all the requirements and that approval by the I.R.S. will be retroactive to include donations made now.) THANK YOU FROM THE DEPTHS OF OUR HEARTS

Peoples Temple hired well-known civil rights attorney Charles R. Garry to defend them in the lawsuits that the Concerned Relatives had filed against them and to represent their members in other civil matters. They interpreted the lawsuits and the negative stories about them in the media as part of a conspiracy to destroy Peoples Temple in the U.S. and in Guyana.

Victims of Conspiracy

"This is an organized, orchestrated, premeditated government campaign to destroy a politically progressive church…"

—*Charles Garry*

YOU CAN NEVER BELIEVE IT—UNTIL IT HAPPENS TO YOU!

Peoples Temple and Rev. Jim Jones have been maligned by some of the news media and have been the brunt of vicious lies for months. The outlandish lies have been carried repeatedly on the front pages of some newspapers, while articles that vindicate us seldom appear anywhere but on the back pages near the obituary column.

We are responsible for saving many lives from drug addiction, crime, and anti-social behavior. Even from terrorism. And taxpayers have been saved perhaps a million dollars a year by the kinds of work we have done with youth headed into delinquency. And yet we are harassed. Obviously, anyone can see the lies perpetrated against us are nothing but a smear.

It is hard to know whom to trust among reporters. Some very responsible and successful reporters know and believe in our good works, but their hands are tied for some reason. We don't even want to ask some reporters who would print the truth about Peoples Temple to come under the kind of harassment it would cause them…the kind of harassment we have been under and endured. In many cases

Victims of Conspiracy

"This is an organized, orchestrated, premeditated, government campaign to destroy a politically progressive church..."

−Charles Garry

YOU CAN NEVER BELIEVE IT — UNTIL IT HAPPENS TO YOU!

Peoples Temple and Rev. Jim Jones have been maligned by some of the news media and have been the brunt of vicious lies for months. The outlandish lies have been carried repeatedly on the front pages of some newspapers, while articles that vindicate us seldom appear anywhere but on the back pages near the obituary column.

We are responsible for saving many lives from drug addiction, crime, and anti-social behavior. Even from terrorism. And taxpayers have been saved perhaps a million dollars a year by the kinds of work we have done with youth headed into delinquency. And yet we are harassed. Obviously, anyone can see the lies perpetrated against us are nothing but a smear.

It is hard to know whom to trust among reporters. Some very responsible and successful reporters know and believe in our good works, but their hands are tied for some reason. We don't even want to ask some reporters who would print the truth about Peoples Temple to come under the kind of harassment it would cause them...the kind of harassment we have been under and endured. In many cases we have remained silent rather than bring the heat of this controversy against us down on some conscientious news reporters.

We are not sure anybody is listening or that many care. We would not be surprised if we were short lived. But this is the way DEMOCRACY DIES, AND WE OWE IT TO THOSE COMING AFTER US TO TELL WHAT CAN HAPPEN TO THEM—whether anybody cares what happens to us or not.

Inside are the facts about a conspiracy against good people. Maybe you can never believe it—UNTIL IT HAPPENS TO YOU!

we have remained silent rather than bring the heat of this controversy against us down on some conscientious news reporters.

We are not sure anybody is listening or that many care. We would not be surprised if we were short lived. But this is the way DEMOCRACY DIES, AND WE OWE IT TO THOSE COMING AFTER US TO TELL WHAT CAN HAPPEN TO THEM—whether anybody cares what happens to us or not.

Inside are the facts about a conspiracy against good people. Maybe you can never believe it—UNTIL IT HAPPENS TO YOU!

State Department Information Sheets
February 28, 1978

The Privacy Act of 1974 limited the amount of information American Embassy officials could reveal about the personal affairs of an American citizen abroad without the individual's consent. In February 1978, the State Department issued several information sheets about Peoples Temple for officials in the U.S. and Guyana to use as guidelines for responding to requests about the custody case of six-year-old Jonestown resident John Stoen, whose parents were former members living in the U.S., and relatives' requests about other Jonestown residents.

INFORMATION SHEET NUMBER 2

ALLEGATIONS OF EMBASSY OR USG INTERFERENCE

All the parties in the custody case of John Victor Stoen, currently in the courts in Guyana, are American citizens. The parents of the child are on one side and the Peoples Temple, a California religious organization which also operates in Guyana, on the other.

Our Ambassador and his staff in Guyana have taken an interest in the case, but have emphasized that the interest of the United States is confined to assuring that the matter is fairly and impartially adjudicated in the courts strictly on its merits and without interference from any quarter. Consistent with this position, the Embassy has avoided taking any sides in what is essentially a civil dispute between two groups of Americans. Nor has any pressure been brought by the Embassy on the Government of Guyana or its courts, which have yet to rule on the matter, in favor of one side or the other.

The inquiries made by the American Embassy on behalf of the child's parents were normal protective services which any American citizen abroad could expect to receive from his government. The inquiries were not attempts to interfere in the internal affairs of Guyana and, indeed, have not been interpreted as such.

INFORMATION SHEET NUMBER 3

PEOPLES TEMPLE GENERAL

As part of the traditional and internationally sanctioned protection services, officers of the American Embassy in Georgetown, Guyana, periodically visit the Peoples Agricultural Temple located at Jonestown, Guyana. These officers have been free to move about the grounds and speak privately to any individuals, including persons who were believed by their family and friends to be held there against their will. It is the opinion of these officers, reinforced by conversations with local officials who deal with the Peoples Temple, that it is improbable anyone is being held in bondage. In general, the people appear healthy, adequately fed and housed and satisfied with their lives on what is a large farm. Many do hard, physical labor but there is no evidence of persons being forced to work beyond their capacity or against their will.

Should you have a specific individual about whom you want information, please provide the name of the person and the person's date and place of birth to the Office of Special Consular Services, Department of State, Washington, D.C. 20520. During the next visit to the Peoples Temple by an officer of the American Embassy, that officer will attempt to speak privately with the individual in question, convey your concern and report to you.

Notes, Letters, and Memos
1977–1978

In Guyana, Peoples Temple carefully documented their meetings with each other and with American and Guyanese officials. They wrote long, detailed analyses of their meetings and reported to Jim Jones on their activities, plans, and observations. In these notes and memoranda, Jonestown residents, including Marceline Jones, wrote to Jim Jones about the challenges they were facing in Jonestown and their concerns for the future.

- In this memo, *Marceline Jones* referred to the screening of Costa-Gavras's 1969 film *Z*. Jonestown residents occasionally watched movies as a community activity. Films and taped television shows that Peoples Temple shipped from the U.S. to Guyana included *The Parallax View, Planet of the Apes, Roots, Catch 22, Klute,* and *Chinatown,* as well as children's programs like *Sesame Street.*

   1. Today on my rounds a little boy asked me to please write Dad a note and ask if they could have open house. After further investigation I learned that the school had planned open house on Sunday from 7 to 9 p.m. It was then postponed until Monday since Peoples' Rally was held. Because of the movie ZEE it could not be held again. I don't know this child's name but it seemed so important to him that I thought it would be important to other children. Maybe if you could let them know you are sensitive to the problem even if it must wait until next Sunday or indefinitely, it would help. *Tom Grubbs would like to do it tomorrow evening if possible.*

   2. I know that every person alive has a saturation point. Some have left at that time. Which is unforgivable. But other of us handle these times in less damaging ways such as withdrawing, crying alone, doing exercise and etc. However, I think that if people could be encouraged rather than discouraged to verbalize their frustrations without feeling they are being judged, we might be able to head off some of the treason and serious acting out. I saw Tom Grubbs today and he seems extremely pleased with how things are going and I hear you handled it very well. I am proposing not that you be burdened with handling these situations, but that a group of counselors be trained to handle them and that people not feel guilty when they express conflict and frustration. Often, just an explanation as to why a thing must be done will suffice. I know this is no panacea. I just did some thinking today after Johnny [Brown] Jones said he wished we could identify people who were having problems before severe acting out occurs.

- *Eugene Chaiken*, an attorney who handled many of the Peoples Temple real estate transactions, referred here to two lawsuits; one initiated by Maria Katsaris's father for libel and slander, and the other filed by former members of Peoples Temple, Wade and Mabel Medlock, who claimed they were coerced into giving their property to the church. Leona, referred to in the first paragraph, worked in the Peoples Temple San Francisco administrative offices.

Jim:

While doing the legal work on the various lawsuits, we have been focusing on the various problems that confront us. The lawsuits are a major issue. They will certainly result in judgments, at least the Katsaris and maybe the Medlock. These judgments will be used to harass as long as we operate in the States. It will cost a whole lot of money to defend them. We don't think it is worth beyond a rear guard type action. The best thing we can do is to sell the remaining three properties we have in the next 90 days for the best price obtainable and get out. If we want to leave Leona and a few back to play church as they might like, that is O.K. till the lawsuits put too much heat on them. But for the most part we think the game is up there.

Of course this leaves us in a severe financial predicament here. The predicament will increase as our population increases. We do not feel that as the community is now structured it can ever be financially self-sufficient (we have put 20 times more effort into band and karate in the last six months than into the construction of a sawmill) and we see that historically small, self-contained communities have always failed. It seems that we spend so much time dealing with day to day tactics, staving off one situation and in the process creating the next, that we do not confront the basic, ultimate problems of our community. In a nutshell, they are that our financial reserves are insufficient to operate on in the long run, that they are being destroyed by inflation, that we are not on our way at all to becoming an economically self-sufficient community and that we will not be such as long as we spend most of our time fighting rear guard actions and we are not sufficiently secure to develop businesses where the money is, namely in Georgetown. So long as we have to cover our ass, so long as P.R. [Public Relations] has priority over production, so long as we are not free to invest and use our money in [George] town, we will not make it here. Unfortunately, time is very much against us now.

Gene Chaiken

▨ *Harriet S. Tropp* wrote this memo to Jim Jones in the fall of 1978, shortly before Don Freed, an American filmmaker, planned to visit Jonestown. Her frustration with the decision-making process in the Jonestown community was further exacerbated by weather in the jungle, which always seemed to confound their expectations.

To: Jim

Re: The Uglification of Jonestown

I hope this doesn't sound like an "I told you so" document but here goes.

Before we started the fiasco of beautifying Jonestown for upcoming guests, advice was given on several different occasions, advice that was the product of several meetings and consultations with people who have lived here for several years as well as Guyanese, to the effect that any attempt to fix the road or haul fines in for the paths would only result in a worsening of the situation if done during the rainy season.

Notwithstanding this advice, we decided to go ahead (and I certainly participated in that decision) and try it anyway because "Dad wants it done" and "there must be a way." Well, there wasn't a way. If you look at the road now, it is worse looking than when we started. If you look at the area by the garden shed, you will see that we have managed to put manganese fines on a path that didn't look bad in the first place, at the expense of destroying what was once one of the prettiest parts of the project…

I think the above just serves to highlight a problem we have in decision-making. That is, if you say you want something done, we ignore any advice we've been given and we go against our own judgment, and go ahead. I know you think that this should not be, but despite what you may think about it, *this is what happens.* We may raise objections, but naturally, because we all follow the procedure of collective decision-making, once a decision is made, even if the wrong one, we try to make it work. But the truth of the matter is that no matter how much you, me or anyone wants something to happen, there are times when it *cannot be done* because of objective conditions.

The cardinal objective condition in the tropics is the weather. You can't fight it. I'm sorry if any of this sounds intemperate, but I am extremely upset at the ugly mess I see we've made of this project, especially with guests coming. *And it was all unnecessary,* if we'd just followed advice…

I think the essence of the problem, or at least one aspect of it, is that no one is willing to oppose your opinion in certain matters, and I frankly think that sometimes you are wrong, and no one is willing to say so. I realize this is quite a volatile statement, but I think it is one factor in the dynamics of how this organization functions that gets us in trouble.

▨ In these two short notes, *Lovie Jean Lucas* explained why she wanted to return to the U.S. and how other Jonestown residents were treating her because she wanted to leave Guyana. Jonestown residents recorded their dissatisfaction with life in Jonestown in letters to Jim Jones and to people who were assigned as counselors. Some members who traveled to Jonestown were expecting to spend only a year there. Others left their homes abruptly and were not prepared for a permanent move to Guyana.

Wed. (I think)

To whom it may concern:

My name is L. Jean Lucas. In the beginning when I arrived here, I asked for a *trip*—*trip* back to take [care] of my unfinished *business,* as I know that the way I had to leave, it did *not* have to be that way—as you can see what developed because of *that.* I am designated as a *liar, thief* and a *traitor,* and I am not guilty of any of this. And there is more, I ask anyone who has any sensitivity, how can I live with *this* and be *happy* or *free?* When I asked for the trip, I know that there are others who have had a trip back to take care of important business so I was told to *WAIT.* It is going onto 2 years, so I am still *waiting.* In fascist countries they say justice *delayed* is *justice denied.* Here we do not use fascist tactics so I am making myself clear. I have only went along with the going back to stay when I was told to *wait.* Whatever has *developed* during my *waiting,* I cannot help *that.*

Thurs. (I think)

Dear Johnny & Ava;

If I am understanding right Dad said over the P.A. that he has made a *new rule* regarding those who wanted to go back to the U.S.A. and for someone to get counsel going or something etc.

Johnny, I do not wish to bring Dad through anything more, I'd rather just get ready and go very soon. I do not think as my mind is bent on going back, that I should stay here any longer than I have to because I know it *hurts Him* and I know it *hurts me.* However whatever is decided for me to do in order to make things right, say if you want counseling o.k. but I do not think it will come out with the truth, and it would not change my mind. Although I would like to give you the whole story before I *leave* just for the *record.*

Johnny, I have looked at every angle of this situation expressible, I am *old* and I have no future *here.* I usually follow my mind and it's hard to "teach an *old* dog new tricks."

Respectfully & Sincerely,

Jean Lucas

P.S. (May I hear from you soon) J.L.

■ After his arrival in Jonestown, Jim Jones had initiated a series of dramatic events that became known as White Nights. At first, the events were set up as defensive responses to what he described as military assaults against the community. He told the residents that outside forces were attacking them for several reasons: to kidnap John Stoen and other children who were involved in custody disputes, to imprison or to kill him, and to torture members of the community because of their political beliefs. Armed with weapons and farming implements, the residents would surround the community and guard it for many hours, often overnight, until Jim Jones declared that the danger had passed.

By 1978, the White Nights included community-wide tests of the Jonestown residents' support for Jim Jones, socialism, and each other. They were asked to articulate their levels of commitment to several plans in the event Jonestown were attacked or forced to leave Guyana, including emigrating to Cuba or the USSR, returning to the United States, relocating only the children and caregivers to another country, and self-annihilation of the community, which Jim Jones referred to as "revolutionary suicide."

In this note to Jim Jones written shortly after a White Night rehearsal in May 1978, *Marceline Jones* asks permission to help implement a plan that would assure the future safety of the children in Jonestown.

May 15, 1978

Jim,

I submit this proposal with the deepest sincerity. I know and hope you will accept it. I've lived long enough. For many years I've lived for just one reason, and that was to safeguard the lives of children. If some asylum could be arranged for our children. Especially the babies and preschool children could be saved for socialism and they are young enough to adjust to a new culture and learn a new language. You and adults of your choosing could go to care for the children and I, with Dr. Schacht, could stay back to see that everyone else was cared for humanely. I've spent much of my life doing what I could to ease suffering in line of my profession. I promise—I will do all I can to relieve all here of their suffering. I do not ask for the lives of my children if you think them unworthy. I do implore you to allow me to do this. It would be my pleasure.

■ By October 1978, as this memo written by *Eugene Chaiken* with *Tom Grubbs* and *Dick Tropp* reflects, Peoples Temple was seriously exploring the possibility of moving the entire community of Jonestown to the USSR. Peoples Temple members in Georgetown were meeting with Soviet Embassy officials and arranging for a delegation from Jonestown to visit the USSR in December 1978. The members were determined to continue their plan to develop a self-sustaining agricultural community.

October 25, 1978

The USSR Possible Settlement Locations, Geography and Climate

1. General Statements and Conclusions:

   All available "southern" areas in the USSR fall in latitudes equivalent to Pittsburgh on the south, Albany in the center, and Montreal on the north. In a generalized sense there are no climates which are warm the year round…

2. Criteria for Evaluation:

   We felt that anywhere citrus crops could be grown it would not be too cold in the winters because the trees can only withstand a small amount of frost. There may be, however, winters with a lot of 45 to 55 degree weather. These we considered "first choice" areas. The next best we felt were areas where rice and cotton are grown, because they take hot summers and fairly long growing seasons…

3. First Choice Areas—Mediterranean Climate, citrus production:

   No. 1. The east coast of the Black Sea, south of the Caucasus Mountains…

   No. 2. An area south of Baku, on the western side of the Caspian Sea…

   No. 3. & 4.: These are located within 300 miles or so of each other, in the foothills or the mountains that make up the northern Himalayas, in the general vicinity of China—Pakistan—Soviet border, south and west of Lake Balkhash.…

4. Second Choice Areas—"Southern" Continental Climate, rice and cotton production:

   These are two areas, quite similar, which follow the river beds of the two main rivers that flow from the mountains in the south, generally north, and empty into the Sea of Aral…

5. Other Choices:

   The best of the rest seem to have a latitude and climate not unlike Minneapolis, Minn. Or colder. Perhaps the areas of Moldavia or the southernmost and westernmost portions of the Ukrainian SSR, right near the Black Sea, might be more mild…

6. Political Evaluation:

It appears less likely that they would be interested in putting us in highly populated, well-developed areas near strategic borders, such as Nos. 1, 2, and the southwest, though No. 1 would appear the best for us. However, they have permitted the settlement in the nearby Armenian SSR of some 200,000 non-Soviet Armenians in the last 20 years. Unfortunately, these "preferred" living areas present the appearance of fairly large population concentrations and full use of the available farmland. We feel, therefore, for both political and demographic reasons that the Soviets would rather have us in a new "pioneering" area—which means Nos. 3 & 4, or the "second choice" areas.

7. Conclusion:

We suggest that the Soviets may not understand our needs for, or rather our standards of a "warm" climate. Our literature is very generalized and we are not able to get good descriptions of small areas. We strongly suggest that a party of our people go to any of the areas suggested by the Soviets, during the winter, to make a firsthand inspection of the conditions and an evaluation of their suitability for our people.

▦ In her 1978 memo to Jim Jones, titled "Analysis of Future Prospects," *Carolyn Layton* reviewed the external and internal pressures on Peoples Temple caused by government investigations into their financial records, pending lawsuits, and living conditions in Jonestown. She questioned the effect of negative publicity on their relationship with the Guyanese government and voiced concern about the financial security of the agricultural project, which was partially dependent on members' Social Security income. In outlining alternatives for the future of Peoples Temple, such as moving to Cuba, paying for the flights of those wanting to return to the U.S., and scaling back the agricultural project, she discussed the possibility of a final stand that would end in the death of the entire Jonestown community.

What I am trying to say is if we make a stand or decide to die how are we going to do it? How would you convince Stephan, or would you? How will we have the knowledge to know now is the time to go ahead and do it? Do you give everyone pills...

Perhaps planning is the answer to all this—maybe there is a practical way all this can be arranged. I wish I knew because there are things I would and should burn and things which should be kept if we choose death. I guess I am so anal that I would like to have everything all organized before I die including what I would like people to come along and find about you and the organization after we are gone. I wish the book were done too. I wish documents could be organized that need to be kept. I guess this is all stupid and unrealistic, but those are some of my feelings on death. I would so much rather have it planned, but like you said, life is cruel and death comes at the very most awful times when a person is totally unprepared or the last moments are so untimely…

One alternative you have never seemed to [have] seriously considered is you and the children going to Cuba, as you could probably could get in there in that small a group. We could try to hold the project together and I would hope that I could see Kimo every now and then and perhaps he could visit here too with me. It would be a hell of a life but at least I suppose the little guys would have a chance and if you made inroads, maybe more could join you there in time. That way they could not get John and if you were not the focal point here, perhaps [U.S.] government agencies would stop honing in on the project here and some heat would be taken off the government here.

I really think Cuba would take you with just your immediate family. The language problem would not be very difficult with your Portuguese.

The project could go on here if it can maintain and if the people leave, then they could just go and we could see what happens. There are a number of people who would love it here if the group size were smaller and more manageable and without crowding, less people to feed, the economic strain would be less. They could not claim that you are taking the money when you are not even here.

I am not saying the group as it now exists could hold together, but a group might and the farm would even have a chance of self-sufficiency.

I could spend some time in both places—Cuba and here if this place needs me, which I suppose it would. We could rotate some.

We would have to close down the US altogether before this would be possible and I know that the order in this place would go to hell without you, but it may go to hell anyway if agencies close in and the government capitulates.

I was just trying to think of a way the little boys could have a dad for a while.

This is probably full of flaws and from my personal point of view I would rather be dead than have this kind of separation, but would do it for the lives of the little guys if there is a possibility that it might work.

Letter to Jim Jones
Congressman Leo J. Ryan
November 1, 1978

A news article about a friend's involvement with Peoples Temple sparked California Congressman Leo J. Ryan's initial interest in Peoples Temple in November 1977. He began interviewing Concerned Relatives and former residents of Jonestown in August 1978. He formally requested congressional approval for a fact-finding mission to Jonestown in October 1978.

Dear Rev. Jones:

In recent months my office has been visited by constituents who are relatives of members of your church and who expressed anxiety about mothers and fathers, sons and daughters, brothers and sisters who have elected to assist you in the development of your church in Guyana.

I have listened to others who have told me that such concerns are exaggerated. They have been supportive of your church and your work. Your effort, involving so many Americans from a single U.S. geographic location, is unique. In an effort to be responsive to these constituents with differing perspectives and to learn more about your church and its work, I intend to visit Guyana and talk with appropriate government officials. I do so as part of my assigned responsibilities as a Member of the House Committee on International Relations. Congressman Ed Derwinski (R-ILL), also a member of the committee, and staff members of the committee will be accompanying me.

While we are in Guyana, I have asked our Ambassador, John Burke, to make arrangements for transportation to visit your church and agricultural station at Jonestown. It goes without saying that I am most interested in a visit to Jonestown, and would appreciate whatever courtesies you can extend to our Congressional delegation.

Please consider this letter to be an open and honest request to you for information about your work which has been the center of your life and purpose for so many years. In the interest of simplifying communications, it will only be necessary for you to respond to Ambassador John R. Burke at the American Embassy in Georgetown. Since the details of our trip are still being arranged, I am sure the Ambassador and his staff will be able to keep you informed.

I look forward to talking with you either in Jonestown or Georgetown.

"Reading and Commentary of the News Today"
Jim Jones
November 9–10, 1978

Jim Jones's announcements to the Jonestown community over the loudspeakers became increasingly difficult to follow as Congressman Ryan's visit drew closer. In these remarks that followed his commentary on current events on November 9 and 10, 1978, Jones reminded the residents of his efforts to protect them and warned them not to leave the community. He also reminded them how he—regardless of the financial cost—had provided the best possible medical care for them. He identified the Klingman child as one of the Jonestown residents who were evacuated for emergency medical treatment and referred to future flights for Jonestown residents who needed medical care that was not available in Guyana.

Remember, we are still in a state of siege. We are going to be under siege beginning Tuesday, when the first of the group we have found will be arriving by commercial airlines. We are hoping and feeling that the Guyana government will block them from staying longer. But they are racial—racist element through and through, though mixed with black and white. They are cooperating with Congressman Ryan, who has voted sharply in racist terms and fascist terms, who is a supporter of Pinochet of Chile. So we will have to be very wise and very alert. Some may be coming by plane. We know those limited number of about 15 that will be arriving Tuesday night by plane. But there's still persistent rumor from our reliable infiltrators that they are planning to come in secretly up river. So we must unify and forget what little differences and disagreements and what we may feel are deprivations and realize that we are under the onslaught of a direct move of a mercenary fascist effort of the United States of America. I love you very deeply and will be seeing you in peoples' rally shortly…

Many of you still have not come to terms, as I said, with imprisonment or death. In all purposes, you would count on victory. You must always be the victor, in order for you to be committed to socialism. You must be always aware of benefits, rather than the fact there can be sacrifices…I find it impossible to expect just good times when Steve Biko was tortured for some six days, night and day, and then drug in a car for 600 miles and his body was hardly nothing left but bones. I could go on and go on and go on. The number that have fallen. Martin Luther King. Malcolm X shot down, his head split open in front of his children in his

Peoples Temple dance performance in San Francisco.
Jim Jones behind podium. MSP 3800

Peoples Temple members printing *Peoples Forum*, newsletter published by Peoples Temple from 1976 to 1978. MSP 3800

Front entrance of the Peoples Temple building in San Francisco at 1859 Geary Boulevard near Fillmore Street. Dozens of members, including Jim Jones's family, lived in small apartments and dormitory rooms on the upper floors. Peoples Temple officially moved its headquarters to San Francisco in 1976. The building was torn down after the 1989 Loma Prieta earthquake. A post office now occupies the site. MSP 3800

Peoples Temple members in Jonestown, Guyana. A small
group of members moved to Guyana in 1974 to clear land
and construct farm buildings and housing. Jim Jones, in hat
and sunglasses, visited the project several times before moving there in the summer of 1977. MSP 3800

Peoples Temple purchased two boats to transport members, supplies, and heavy machinery in Guyana. The *Cudjoe* was a seventy-two-foot trawler that carried members on the overnight trip from Guyana's capital to Jonestown, located in a remote jungle near the Guyana–Venezuelan border.

Peoples Temple members on their way to Guyana. Jim Jones in hat and sunglasses. MS 3800

Peoples Temple members loading a packed crated outside the Redwood Valley church. Members built their own crates—large and small—for shipments of supplies and personal items to Guyana. MSP 3800

Pop Jackson, one of the first settlers in Jonestown.
MSP 3803

Pop Jackson with his wife, Luvenia, in Jonestown. MSP 3803

Peoples Temple members in Jonestown. MSP 3803

Peoples Temple members in communal kitchen in Jonestown. MSP 3803

thirties. I cannot think that I am above these people, so I am prepared for anything today or tomorrow might bring…

Thank you for your commitment to socialism. I hope you are giving it with a full dedication, not based on benefits, but based upon rightness; not based on living forever, because great socialists like Paul Robeson who gave the most courageous moments of their existence could not live in America. When he came home because of a needy sister in Philadelphia and tried to help her, he could not last one year. America's racism, its apathy, its violence drove him mad, though he was a man who had his senses all of his life, all of his 70 years. But he died in less than a year in Philadelphia, Pennsylvania, after enjoying peace, security and all opportunities of work and recreation in the Soviet Union for many years. This is a picture that has not clearly enough come home to many of you who are citizens of Jonestown; that USA is an imperialist cancer, a disease that has reached out and managed to cause two out of three babies to go to bed hungry, that some people in the United States might be able to have a television, a car to pacify them for the moment, to keep them asleep, like the pig ready for the slaughter. Because the slaughter will come, because the US dollar is falling, the economics of capitalism are indeed in their final stages…Thank you for your attention. I love you very much and do a great deal of reading and studying. And look for Teresa's implementation and Tropp's implementation of the news also in tonight's classes…

Attention, for perhaps one of the most important announcements you have ever heard. I am giving you the free night that I just authorized spoken over this medium. I urge however that you do not wander in any way out of the central area of community, and keep a strict curfew after the entertainment…

You do not know what you are dealing with. I'm the greatest friend you will ever have and I am trying on every level to protect this community. But I warn you, do not, at all times, try to go out in the unknown areas now. They could be even lurking. The airplane that flew so low yesterday trying to determine my location for kidnapping purposes. Truly we have power in our unity, but so many of you are always looking back. You weaken the power that I can give you on the extra plane, the higher plane. You've got to be very grateful now and very joyous and very friendly and very warm with each other. Unfortunately, a number of backbiting and complaining has brought an undue amount of illness upon some of you. So I encourage you, from a heart that will never ever be seen like my heart again, a heart that loves you and cares for you to the very fullest degree, a heart that sent our precious Klingman child clear across the continent of South America [so] that he could get medication before it would be too late—that he would be permanently a cripple and blind and then deaf. We see him return to our midst a totally renewed person practically and the renewal will continue. These plane fares to other countries are fantastically heavy on us. We have seven more that are scheduled. So we want to be sure that we are very, very grateful; that you are looking for every point of gratitude so that the mind is high and the faith is right, because I can reach you for love and protection no more than you allow me to reach you for love and protection. I can reach you in justice and judgment, but that's not my concern. I love you. I have no intention or desire to hurt you. I do have to protect the community against one or two individuals, if they intend to try to hurt the best thing that ever happened to us, as our precious sister sang so beautifully last evening, "Over Yonder."

And I want to remind you, this is a free night. I'm trying to reduce tensions. It's very dangerous to reduce structure and loosen structure when we are under attack. Their plans for the mercenaries, we do not know. We don't know if it is taking place now, or if it will start when the legal actions start, I mean their legal entry, which can't be denied, because the ones that are coming have not been in any trouble currently with the law, though some of our ex-members, and plenty of them have been. So I wanted to warn you again and again and again, to be together with the community, to stay in the sight of the community, do not leave the central area, do not get away from this circle of protection.

Five

The Day of Departure and Death

The week before Congressman Leo J. Ryan planned to visit Jonestown, hundreds of Jonestown residents, almost everyone who could write their names, signed a petition printed on enormous pieces of paper:

Resolution of the Community

Many of us, the undersigned residents of Jonestown, Guyana, have been visited here by our friends and relatives. However, we have not invited and do not care to see Congressman Ryan (supporter of military aid to the Pinochet regime of Chile), media representatives, members of a group of so-called "concerned relatives," or any other persons who may be traveling with, or associated with, any of those persons.

Dated: This 9th day of November, 1978, Jonestown Guyana.

That same week, Jonestown residents rehearsed for the winter holiday show they were scheduled to present in Georgetown in December. Marceline Jones's parents were visiting Jonestown from Indiana. They left midweek. The Jonestown basketball team traveled to Georgetown for their first tournament with a Guyanese team. Reports on all aspects of community life were turned in—agricultural, medical, school, and procurement. In San Francisco, Peoples Temple members were planning a December 5 benefit dinner featuring local politicians and planning another issue of their newspaper, *Peoples Forum*.

Jim Jones saw Congressman Ryan's visit as an intrusion and an act of escalation in Peoples Temple's conflicts with the Concerned Relatives and the media. Others saw the visit as an opportunity for them to show the world, as Peoples Temple attorney Charles Garry put it, "a community life where there's no selfishness, there's no sexism, there's no racism, there's no elitism, and there's no poverty."

While Peoples Temple members prepared for visitors, they continued their efforts to prevent Congressman Ryan from coming into the community. Some residents welcomed the diversion of these preparations so that they could leave Jonestown under cover of all the activity. Others saw the impending visit as their chance to return to the U.S. with the protection of the U.S. government and the media.

The following deposition, report, and transcript reveal parts of the story of the tragic events of November 18.

from Deposition, *Peoples Temple v. Attorney General of California*
J. Evans
April 4, 1982

On the morning of November 18, 1978, three families living in Jonestown walked out of the community and hiked through the jungle toward Matthews Ridge, a town twenty-five miles away. One of the two men in the group, J. Evans, gave this account of their efforts to return to the U.S. in a deposition for *Peoples Temple v. Attorney General of California*, a case related to the dissolution of the church.

Q. If you could basically describe for me your journey through the jungle on November 18th.

A. Okay. Started in the morning, well, the night before, I'll start there.

[My wife] and I talked, and I suggested to her that we should write a note and try to give it to the congressman or give it to somebody who was there.

We hadn't, at that point, seen anyone. We didn't know who it was going to be, but we knew somebody was coming from the States. I said if we could get them a note, and I wrote the note.

She said, no, that's too dangerous. So I canceled that idea.

The following morning, there was an announcement that nobody was to leave. As a matter of fact, they was going to nail the doors so that nobody that was visiting could come—could come eventually to our house and see something they weren't supposed to—the living conditions, actually.

So something changed. The following morning, they didn't nail the houses. They just sent security around that said that we were going to have breakfast. We were going to have a good breakfast, and we were supposed to dress for the occasion and be at our best, and everybody should look happy, you know.

So I told [my wife] I said, "I am packing, you know." The night before, we packed, you know. We didn't write the note. We wrote the note. And I destroyed the note. I think I just chewed it up and swallowed it.

We packed a little green satchel—scout satchel—we had. I put some toothpaste and things that we were going to need because I was ready to go, you know.

So I called all my kids up and, you know, took [my daughter] up to the loft and told her, "We've got to get out of here. I don't know how you feel. As a matter of fact, I don't care how you feel, because when I go, you're going, if I have to drag you out of here."

So at that point, she said, "I've been wanting to go all the time," you know, she said, "But you know how this is, if you talk about something over here, you know what that can do for you."

"I know. I know. You want to go, there's nothing I can do, but now there is something I can do. Somebody is coming in. This is our chance to go." You know.

So the next morning, I went to work. [My wife] and I, we go to work together. We walked down the trail. We got to the medical office, and I saw Richard [Clark].

So when I saw Richard, he looked up at me. I looked at him and that morning, I was dead serious. I had a screwdriver on my belt, right here (indicating). That meant I was ready to go out of there, and if they tried to stop me with guns or whatever, I was going to defend myself.

So I did like that and showed him. He said like that (indicating). So later on, Diane went to [my wife] and told [her] said she wanted to leave and she was going to leave. If we wanted to go, to get ready because Leslie was going. She and Richard were going, and they had already talked about it, and if we wanted to come along and bring all the kids, you know—oh, God, I couldn't believe my ears.

So I went to the school, and I talked to Ms. Johnson, tall lady. She was the principal of the school. I said, "Ms. Johnson," I said, "we want to take [my daughters] out of school today. We want to go on a picnic."

This was a big day. That's where she slipped up. She wasn't supposed to let nobody go. We went to this young teenage lady that was checking everybody— where was this person to go and whatever. DeeDee let us go, which was a friend of [my wife] you know. They used to come over to our house in the States and all that. So we had good rapport with her.

She let us go. She signed us out. And we started walking. Here we are, walking out of town, you know, scared to look back. So we walked out. And when we got to the jungle—not the jungle, per se, in the thickness of the jungle, but on the clay trail. We just kept straight on out and kept walking.

So by the time we got to the gate, we were not only to the gate, we were a few feet from the gate. I saw this tractor-trailer coming into town with a couple of people we knew from town. The weirdest thing, they looked at us and just waved, you know, a real trance-like appearance on their face. It wasn't emotional at all. No emotion.

This guy that was waving at me, this guy is really jovial, always happy, always joking, real rebellious against Jones, all the time. He was nothing that day. I mean, I saw him, he had no emotion. He was just (indicating).

I waved at him and I just kept walking, you know. We just kept walking as if we was going to a picnic. After they passed, we kept walking. We heard another tractor-trailer coming from the opposite direction going towards the gate. That's when we ducked to the bushes. I mean, you know, there's got to be somebody looking for us, and we were past the point where we was supposed to go.

So we ducked in the bushes. I went—and we couldn't find the trail that led from the jungle to the railroad tracks—so I went looking for the trail. I got lost, you know. I did everything I could, cut the bushes to remind and got lost.

So I'm cutting back—trying to get back to them—and I cut right up on them. Here they are, standing.

So it started raining, and we had the kids. I just picked the kids up, my kids, my two little babies. I had both of them walking through the water, trying to get out to the tracks.

So once we made it to the tracks, Leslie said, "Let's go to Port Kaituma. It's only seven miles from here."

I said, "No, let's go the opposite direction because they're going to expect us to go the shortest distance," you know. The other way was like—I'm not really certain—but I know when we looked at the sign, it said eighteen miles. That's how far we had walked at that point. We walked a little further because the train was late. Anyway, I'll get back to that.

So we didn't go the Port Kaituma route and had we went that route, we would have been dead. Again, you know.

So what we did, we went down the tracks a long distance, the twenty-two miles or whatever it was. I had been through there before—I had rode the train through the jungle before. Once we sung at a nightclub, and we came back through the jungle on this freight train. I remembered that. I was trying to get to that train. When we made it there, we walked down the tracks I don' t know how long.

It started raining. We had some pancakes I had saved from breakfast [that] I put in a plastic bag on my belt for the kids. So I gave them all the pancakes I had. We needed some water, so Richard and I climbed down in a ditch and got some water.

So we kept walking and we kept walking.

Leslie had her baby in a sheet on her back, and that kept coming out. So we tied that. And Richard kept changing the babies around. Richard would hold one baby, then we changed around so we could rest up and worked together and walked those miles.

Now, when we got on the train and we finally made it to Matthews Ridge, when we got to Matthews Ridge, the policeman said, "Where you people come from?" So we told them we came from Jonestown. We was escaping. We just had got away. We wanted them to help us if they could help us get back to the United States.

They said, "Do you know what is happening out there?" People are shooting and people are just getting killed. They sent a lot of people out in the jungle.

I said, "What are you talking about?" you know, and he told us. He said, "There's some men from the United States came in, and they shot them and lots of people have been killed." He said, "You come in, come in here right now." So we went in, and they called in these soldiers and put them around the house, all the military.

So we're in this house, and I'm scared to death, you know, because I don't know what has happened. I know [my wife's] sister is there, you know, and we couldn't find out anything.

So they told us, they said, "We'll try to get you some food," you know. They came up with some rice and stuff and fed us. They kept asking all these questions about what was happening and was he crazy or what caused him to act that way. What caused him to do this to all these people.

It went on and on and on. We had no way of finding out from the news or anything, you know, what was happening.

So a few days later, I forget how many days, we went to Georgetown. They rushed us out, and they had, you know, this airplane waiting for us. We just jetted on the airplane and got off and all this military out there with machine guns and this and that. This was really getting us nervous, you know.

So we stayed at this hotel. They moved us from this hotel to this hotel, fearing that somebody would try to get us because we had escaped.

I found out that we were just hours, I guess, away from getting killed, from being right in the middle of that. After we got there, we found that out. That was a shock to us, with all these kids. We came right through the middle of all of that.

The people we told our story to, they couldn't believe it, you know, until they finally had someone to substantiate it. Like Stanley Clayton, all these people that knew us. The day before, everything was normal. We were working everyday in the medical department. He said he had my jacket that I wore to work that morning.

I said, "Hey, man. How did you get my jacket?"

He started crying and we all hugged each other, so glad to see each other, you know.

---

from "Report on CODEL Ryan's Visit to Jonestown and Subsequent Murder"
Richard A. Dwyer
November 22, 1978

In April 1978, Richard A. Dwyer joined the staff of the American Embassy in Georgetown, Guyana, with the title of deputy chief of mission. He visited Jonestown in May 1978 and again in November 1978, this time with Congressman Ryan. He dictated this report on November 20, 1978.

From: American Embassy Georgetown

To: Secretary of State Washington DC

There follows a report of American Embassy Georgetown DOM [Deputy Chief of Mission] Richard A. Dwyer, Control Officer for CODEL RYAN, of the visit of Congressman Ryan to the Peoples Temple Agricultural Community at Jonestown, in northwest Guyana, and the subsequent murder of Congressman Ryan and four other Americans at the airstrip in Port Kaituma. The account begins with the group's departure from Timerhi Airport in Georgetown on Friday, November 17 and concludes with the return of the bodies of the slain Americans toward dusk of Sunday, November 19.

Limited official use

Begin text:

1. Congressman Ryan's party departed from Timerhi Airport Friday, Nov 17 at approximately 1400 hours. The group had no absolute assurances from the Peoples Temple that it would be received at the Peoples Temple Agricultural community in Jonestown before its departure.

2. The group consisted of Congressman Ryan; his aide, Ms. Jackie Speier; and myself, Counselor of Embassy Richard Dwyer, the escort officer to Congressman Ryan; four concerned relatives, Mrs. Oliver, Ms. Carol Boyd,

Mr. Jim Cobb and Mr. Anthony Katsaris; two lawyers for Peoples Temple, Mr. Mark Lane and Mr. Charles Garry; and eleven newsmen, including a four-man NBC news team headed by Mr. Bob Flick and including Messrs. Bob Brown, Don Harris and Steve Sung; Mr. Lindsay of the *National Enquirer,* Mr. Charles Krause of the *Washington Post,* Mr. Greg Robinson and Mr. Tim Reiterman of the *San Francisco Examiner,* and Mr. Ron Javers of the *San Francisco Chronicle.* We were also accompanied by Ministry of Information Officer Neville Annibourne.

3. Shortly before the plane's approach to Port Kaituma, the Pilot, Captain Spence, informed me he had had a radio call from the tower in Georgetown conveying a message from the Peoples Temple in Jonestown that the Port Kaituma airstrip was not serviceable and was unsafe. The group discussed the possibility of going into Matthews Ridge; however, Captain Spence suggested making a pass at the runway at Port Kaituma to determine its condition. The strip appeared in good condition and we went into Port Kaituma where the plane landed at about 1530. Captain Spence informed me later that a fellow pilot had gone into Port Kaituma earlier in the day and had had no reports on runway difficulties.

4. The group was met by about six Peoples Temple representatives upon our descent from the plane. The Peoples Temple representatives were uncommunicative to most of the group and drew aside to talk with their two lawyers. The lawyers announced that the Peoples Temple had decided that the two lawyers should go to Jonestown and confer with Jim Jones on whether the remainder of group would be allowed to enter Jonestown. It was pointed out to the members of the Peoples Temple and their lawyers that the plane had to leave Point Kaituma before darkness at about 6:00 p.m. The two counsels then departed with members of the Peoples Temple in the large truck which was used to traverse the bad road in to the Temple. This and the Peoples Temple tractor were purported to be the only vehicles in the area able to make the trip. A few minutes later, however, the truck reappeared and the lawyers announced that it had been decided that the Congressman, his aide, Ms. Speier, and myself would be permitted to accompany the group. After several delays, including one delay necessary to remove from the Jonestown road a two-wheel cart loaded with heavy logs, the group entered Jonestown about 1630 or 1700 hours. After talks with Jim Jones and other leaders of the Peoples Temple, during which Congressman Ryan expressed the opinion that free entry to and egress

from Jonestown were essential to prove that Jonestown is an open and free community, Jim Jones reluctantly agreed, upon the urging of counsel, to permit the newsmen and the concerned relatives to enter Jonestown.

5. The truck was sent to fetch the newsmen and the concerned relatives. It was agreed that the Congressman's party would pass the night at Jonestown while the remainder of the group would have dinner at Jonestown but spend the night at Port Kaituma and return the following morning. While awaiting the press and concerned relatives to arrive, Congressman Ryan and his aide, Ms. Speier, began interviewing the numerous residents of Jonestown about whom they had had inquiries or other reports. With the arrival of the newsmen supper was served to the visitors and a number of the leaders of Jonestown. The newsmen were able to speak with Jim Jones and others for some considerable time.

6. It was announced that following supper a musical show would be presented by the "Jonestown Express," a group preparing for its annual Christmas concert in Jonestown. Mrs. Jones announced to the assembled group that no one need be photographed if they did not wish to be, that the NBC team would be using bright lights and television cameras and that if anyone did not wish to be photographed, they should raise their hands and the lights would be turned off and the TV cameras turned away from them. As the concert progressed, however, I observed no incidents of people refusing to be photographed. The musical show contained considerable talent and the people of Jonestown were very enthusiastic throughout the show and in apparent good humor.

7. Midway in the show Mrs. Jones got up and warmly introduced Congressman Ryan, who came to the stage to say a few words. The Congressman noted he had already met at Jonestown some of his former students, a school classmate of his daughter's, and others with whom he had mutual friends or acquaintances. He said that he had already talked to a considerable number of residents of Jonestown and he was happy to hear that a number of these people felt that Jonestown was the greatest place on earth, upon which statement the audience rose with enthusiastic and prolonged applause. Congressman Ryan then went back to his interviewing and the show progressed. The Congressman continued interviewing persons on his list, in private following the show.

8. At the end of the evening I was approached by Mr. Vern Gosney, who asked me if I could arrange for him to get out of Jonestown that night, as he was

very, very frightened and was afraid that once he had been seen talking to me he would be in extreme danger. I replied that I could do nothing that night as I myself was staying at Jonestown but that Mr. Gosney, if that was his wish, was welcome to leave Jonestown in the morning with the group. I noted that Mr. Jones and his legal counsel had assured the Congressman, the newsmen and myself that anyone who wished to leave with us was free to leave Jonestown. At about the same time, Mr. Gosney had slipped a note to one of the NBC crew saying that he and Miss Monica Bagby wanted to leave.

9. At the conclusion of the evening's interviewing, Congressman Ryan and I discussed the situation. Miss Bagby and Mr. Gosney were two persons who had clearly expressed the desire to depart, and the Congressman thought that there might be others on his list of names to interview who also wished to depart. He noted he was saving his best-documented cases for the morning. It was therefore agreed that Miss Bagby and Mr. Gosney would be put on the Congressman's list with those about whom the most serious concerns had been expressed and that they would be called for interviews by the Congressman towards the end of the next morning, as shortly as possible before the group was scheduled to depart. The Congressman and I agreed that despite Mr. Jones' assurances that people would be free to leave, there might be concern among the Peoples Temple when it became apparent that some members were preparing to depart.

10. Next morning, Saturday, Nov 18, the Congressman began the remainder of his interviews. The news group returned and also began interviewing leaders and members of the Peoples Temple. In the meantime, the Peoples Temple had given permission for one or two other concerned relatives then in Georgetown to come to Jonestown with the plane that was to pick up the Congressman's group and to spend some time in Jonestown with their relatives before returning to Georgetown by commercial means. The Congressman and I agreed that this was undesirable. I explained on the radio to Consul Ellice and to the Congressman's HIRC [House International Relations Committee] aide, Mr. James Schollaert, the decision that there should be no concerned relatives on the plane that went up to Port Kaituma to pick up the Congressman and his party.

11. The NBC television news crew had also decided to tape its principal interview with Jim Jones shortly before departure Saturday.

12. At approximately 11:00, after consulting with Congressman Ryan, I called

Jim Jones and his lawyers aside and informed them that there would be several people who wanted to leave Jonestown and that these people would depart with the Congressman and myself. Jones was visibly upset but was calmed by Mr. Lane and Mr. Garry, who pointed out that it appeared that only a half dozen to a dozen people wished to depart, which in its way was a credit to a community of 1100 to 1200 people. Congressman Ryan also stressed to Mr. Jones that unhindered departures would improve the image and reputation of the Peoples Temple.

13. By approximately noon, in addition to Miss Bagby and Mr. Gosney, several members of the Parks family had expressed a desire to leave and were holding a family council to decide whether they should all depart together or whether some might remain in Jonestown. It was about 1330 when they decided that they would all depart at the same time with the Congressman and myself and had collected their belongings. Congressman Ryan and Ms. Speier went with members of the Parks family to reassure them while they collected their belongings. The family consisted of grandmother, parents and four children and Mr. O'Neill, a close friend of daughter Brenda Parks. It was apparent by this time that a second aircraft in addition to Otter (which would hold 19 persons) would be needed and was requested by the Peoples Temple radio. A small aircraft of 5-passenger capacity was therefore sent up from Georgetown scheduled with the otter to arrive in Port Kaituma at 2:00, according to messages received from Georgetown. As the departure time from Jonestown came closer, there were several other persons who expressed a desire to leave to the Congressman and myself. It was agreed that the people from Jonestown would be given priority on the planes and that the press and Mr. Garry, who wished to return to Georgetown, would take subsequent aircraft. In addition to the Parks family, the Bogue family, consisting of Jim Bogue, Mr. Bogue, Tina and Tommy, and a close family friend, Harold Cordell, were to leave with the group. At the last moment, Mr. Larry Layton urgently requested that he be permitted to leave and he entered the truck.

14. Congressman Ryan stated that as there were apparently still others who might wish to leave Jonestown, he and I would remain in Jonestown to insure their departure the following day. I was to accompany the departing group to the airport at Port Kaituma to oversee the departures and to relate to the captain of the GAC aircraft the requirements for aircraft the following day. I was also to stop at the assistant district officer's office at

Port Kaituma to relate these messages through that channel to assure prompt and accurate receipt by the Embassy.

15. The group was loaded in the back of the large truck. I got on last. The truck started to depart but slid in the mud at the side of the track. The group was told that a bulldozer would be necessary to put it back on the track. (A previous delay had occurred which Ms. Speier attributed to the fact that the driver of the truck wanted to leave with the group and refused to drive the truck out unless he could be given assurance that he could leave. He was told that he could leave with the group the next day.) As the group waited for the bulldozer to come to free the truck, shouts were heard from the central pavilion of Jonestown where Congressman Ryan was waiting together with Mr. and Mrs. Jones, Mr. Garry, Mr. Lane and other ranking individuals of the Peoples Temple. I ran from the truck to the pavilion, where I found a small group surrounding the Congressman, whose clothes were disheveled and bloody. He had been attacked by a knife-bearing distraught member of the Peoples Temple who had been disarmed by Mr. Lane, Mr. Garry and others. The Congressman was uninjured. I was told that the blood had come from a minor wound the assailant had suffered as the knife was taken from him. The Congressman told Jim Jones that the incident would present a problem for the Peoples Temple but that it was not one which could not be overcome if legal processes were allowed to take place. Jim Jones expressed the wish that he himself had been killed directly on the spot rather than that this incident should happen to the Congressman. He said that the police had been called. He appeared deeply troubled. The Congressman and I had a private conversation in which I urged the necessity for the Congressman to leave Jonestown. The Congressman agreed, finally, to do so, with the understanding that I would return to Jonestown and organize the departure of those who wished to depart the following day. The Congressman and I then joined the truck, which by this time had been freed from the mud, and proceeded to the airport at Port Kaituma approximately an hour away.

16. The truck stopped for a few moments at the entrance to Jonestown, where it was joined by a guard from the gate, who made a careful survey of the passengers in the truck without speaking. Although the two aircraft had been scheduled to arrive at Port Kaituma at 1400, they were not there when the group arrived, about 1530. During the trip out, incidentally, several members of the group leaving Jonestown expressed to me and others their

concern that one Larry Layton had been permitted to join the group, as they considered him a fanatic follower of Mr. Jones and did not believe that he actually wished to leave the organization.

17. Upon arrival at the airport I asked Congressman Ryan to be sure all members of the group were thoroughly searched before being allowed to board the aircraft...And to pay particular attention to Larry Layton, about whom we had been warned.

18. As there was no aircraft in sight upon the group's reaching Port Kaituma airfield (except for the disabled Guyanese Defense Force "Islander" under repair by four GDF members), the GOG Information officer, Mr. Annibourne, who had accompanied the group throughout, and I asked the Peoples Temple driver to take us up to the district office at Port Kaituma to see if we could get in touch with Georgetown by radio to determine what had happened to the planes. I also wished to relay as quickly as possible an account of the attack at Jonestown on Congressman Ryan. We reached the district office only to be told that Assistant District Officer Thomas was across the way at a small establishment. As Mr. Annibourne and I were conversing with Mr. Thomas, relating the events of the day to him and asking that Georgetown and the police be contacted immediately, the two planes were sighted overhead preparing to land at Port Kaituma. The large Jonestown truck immediately turned around and departed for the airport, to the surprise of Mr. Annibourne and myself. We therefore prevailed upon Thomas for transportation to the airport, which was supplied in the person of Mr. Jeffrey Semple, a local businessman and his truck. An individual with a shotgun, whom I took to be a police constable, although he was in mufti, also got into the back of the truck. Mr. Semple, accompanied by Mr. Thomas and Mr. Semple's two small children, drove Mr. Annibourne and me to the airport, where the process of loading the airplanes had already begun. The journalists were still on the ground, as they wished to film the departure and as not all of them could be accommodated in the two aircraft. The Congressman was also on the runway. After a brief conversation with the Congressman regarding the number of people who might wish to depart the following day, I walked over to discuss arrangements with Captain Spence, the pilot of the GAC aircraft, which was mid-way down the airstrip. The five-seat Cessna was near the head of the runway, close to the disabled GDF Islander.

19. Shortly thereafter shots rang out from a tractor and two trailers belonging

to the Peoples Temple which had been parked at the side of the runway nearest the aircraft. Congressman Ryan ran under the nose of the aircraft to get away from the shots coming from the tractor and two trailers, as did I. I saw the Congressman hit once and go down, apparently attempting to seek shelter behind the wheels of the aircraft. I also saw that one or two others of the group had already been hit. I therefore threw myself on the ground on my back to simulate death. As I was falling I was hit by a slug from what was apparently a small caliber weapon, possibly a .22, in my left thigh. The firing continued for several minutes and there was a short pause before the firing recommenced. It seemed to me that one or more of the assailants with shotguns was proceeding amongst the wounded, firing a blast at each of them. For unknown reasons, I was not shot. The truck and tractor were heard to drive away and after a few moments those who had not been wounded and the ambulatory wounded began to get to their feet. The pilots of the otter aircraft, still in the cockpit, had not been attacked and the engines of the plane were still running. I went over to the Congressman, who had been badly hit. It was clear that he was dead. I then moved the body away from under the wheels of the aircraft and checked on the others. The NBC newsmen, Bob Brown and Don Harris, were both lying dead under and to the rear of the aircraft. I ran around to the steps of the aircraft where Mr. Greg Robinson of the *San Francisco Examiner* lay crumpled, also apparently killed instantly. I cannot recall whether I first saw Ms. Jackie Speier still on board the aircraft or at the foot of the steps. It appeared evident, however, that she was seriously wounded, as was Mr. Anthony Katsaris, who lay near the foot of the aircraft steps. I ran up the steps of the aircraft, where I found that Ms. Patricia Parks had received what appeared to be the full blast of a shotgun in the back of her head. She was leaning across the aisle of the airplane. With the help of a local Amerindian who appeared on the scene I removed the body from the aircraft in the hope that the aircraft could still fly, but only then noted that the left-hand tires had been shot out. I do not recall seeing any other passengers on the aircraft and presumed they had run towards the heavy bush on the near side of the runway. Those remaining unhurt and some local residents carried Mr. Katsaris, Ms. Speier and NBC newsman Stephen Sung, also seriously injured, into the bush at the side of the runway.

20. The major concern of the group was that the Peoples Temple assailants might return to finish the assassination. The wounded were therefore

moved into the bush and those able to walk stayed near the bush. Mr. Bob Flick of the NBC news team, who had taken shelter in a small corrugated steel building at the side of the runway with several Guyanese and was not injured by the gunfire directed towards him, ran down the runway to where the other light plane was. There were four members of the GDF at the disabled GDF Islander, three of whom had automatic weapons and the commanding officer, Lt. Joseph, who had an automatic pistol. Lt. Joseph later told me that none of his group had discharged their weapons because they could not tell the assailants from the victims, as all were Americans and the incident was over so quickly.

21. Mr. Fernandes, the pilot of the Cessna, joined the group near the Otter, where he told me that one of his passengers had attempted to kill the other passengers with a revolver and had seriously wounded at least two. Mr. Dale Parks, who had been a passenger on Mr. Fernandes' Cessna, told me the passengers consisted of Miss Monica Bagby, Mr. Vern Gosney, Mr. Larry Layton, himself and one other. He stated as the Cessna was preparing to depart, Mr. Layton shot Miss Bagby and Mr. Gosney once each in the back. The door of the plane was opened and Miss Bagby and Mr. Gosney ran out of the plane and were shot again, once each, by Mr. Layton, who then turned the gun on Mr. Parks. Mr. Parks stated that there was one further discharge of the weapon but that he was not injured and was able to take the weapon away from Mr. Layton after a struggle and attempt to discharge it at Mr. Layton, without result. Layton then is said to have disappeared temporarily. One of the GDF soldiers stationed by the GDF aircraft under repair near the Cessna later told me that he thought Mr. Layton had left the area with the Peoples Temple. Subsequently, however, Mr. Layton was identified by several members of the Parks family and others mingling with the group of survivors at the side of the runway near the disabled Otter.

22. By the time I had taken possession of the revolver from Mr. Parks and one round of ammunition which Mr. Parks said had apparently failed to fire, two Guyanese in civilian clothes asserting that they were associated with the Guyanese authorities had hold of Mr. Layton and said that they would escort him to jail.... At about this time the Cessna aircraft began to take off, apparently containing Captain Spence from the GAC Otter and his co-pilot, and pilot Fernandes. As the aircraft began to take off I ran toward it to flag it down so as to take out some of the wounded. Captain Spence gestured to the

rear of the aircraft, which I took to mean that there had been another appearance of the group from the Peoples Temple and the survivors and I therefore once again took to the bush. I was later to learn that Captain Spence apparently was gesturing to the badly wounded Monica Bagby, whom they had on board.

23. Numerous Guyanese approached the survivors cautiously. We prevailed upon one individual with a Land Rover to request help from the clinic in Port Kaituma, painkillers at the very least. And hopefully means of transportation for the wounded to the clinic. The individual did return, stating that all residents of Port Kaituma had been ordered to stay indoors. That the practitioners were afraid to help the survivors to the center of Port Kaituma, which they felt in any event might be unsafe. The man did, however, deliver a package of painkillers.

24. It should be noted that before Captain Spence's departure and while he was in radio contact with Guyanese authorities elsewhere, either in Matthews Ridge or Georgetown, he assured me that assistance would be immediately on the way. This was at approximately 1630 hours, which meant that there should have been time for an aircraft to reach Port Kaituma from Georgetown before night had it left immediately. With this assurance the group assembled by the edge of the runway. Several individuals were missing—Mr. James Cobb, Mr. O'Neill, the Parks children, Tracy and Brenda, and the Bogue children, Tina and Tommy. They had run deep into the bush and could not be located. I talked with the lieutenant in charge of the small detachment at the GDF plane at the head of the runway, requesting the cots of the four-man detachment to be used as stretchers. The lieutenant agreed that the wounded could be brought to his four-man unit's tent but recommended that this be done after dark. In hopes that an aircraft might still arrive, the group remained close to the bush near the Otter with wounded hidden in the bush until after 2000 [hours], when the wounded were carried down to the GDF tent, where they were made as comfortable as possible. The wounded consisted of Ms. Speier, Mr. Sung, Mr. Katsaris and Mr. Gosney, who had been located lying wounded in the bush by some Amerindians. It should be noted that several residents of the area were of great assistance to the group. They warned us of possibility of attack from the far end, helped carry the wounded and helped search for those lost in the bush.

25. At this point the decision had to be made whether to attempt to keep the

ambulatory members of the group together in one place to facilitate their departure should transportation arrive, or whether it would be safer to attempt to scatter them, either in the bush or amongst the houses of inhabitants living near the airport, if possible. I selected the former option and with the assurances of Mr. Semple that his family would welcome the group, two persons were left to stay with the wounded and the rest of the group assembled in Mr. Sempel's tavern about one block from the head of the runway. Mr. Sempel offered the use of his living quarters for the group, which were above the tavern proper and where the group gratefully assembled. The normal Saturday night activities of the tavern continued below, in some measure serving as a camouflage for the group.

26. About 2300 hours Assistant District Officer Thomas appeared at the tavern to state that he had just come out of the bush where he had taken cover when the shots began. He said he had been in touch with the authorities by radio from his office in Port Kaituma and that an aircraft would be sent in shortly to be guided by lighted oil pots alongside the runway. This tactic had apparently been used in the past by the Peoples Temple when they had an urgent need for medical evacuations at night. Mr. Thomas and I returned to the airport to discuss with Lt. Joseph of the four-man detachment the placing of the oil lights, and awaited the aircraft.

27. Mr. Thomas returned to his office. It became apparent that the aircraft would not come in that night. Mr. Bob Flick of NBC refused to leave the wounded and nursed them to the best of his ability throughout the night. I also stayed with the wounded to be on hand at the arrival of the first aircraft after instructing the group at the tavern that no one was to leave under any conditions unless Mr. Flick, myself or a GOG official gave permission, whether or not an aircraft was heard to land.

28. At approximately 0130 or 2000 in the morning a message came from Lt. Joseph that there was a radio telephone message in . . .

29. A company of troops, approximately 120 men, were being sent from Mathews Ridge to Port Kaituma by rail but they had orders to dismount five miles before Port Kaituma and walk in. The first troops arrived about 0630, just after dawn . . . one hour later the full company was on hand guarding the perimeters of the airport and six soldiers with automatic weapons were assigned to the tavern to guard the Americans staying there. A paramedic arrived with the troops and assisted the wounded.

30. The first rescue aircraft arrived at approximately 0945–1000 in the morning.

It arrived without any medical facilities, without stretchers, without blankets, without mattresses. The three most seriously wounded were laid on the bare floor of the cabin, from which the seats had been removed, and two others, less seriously wounded and who could sit, were also put in the aircraft and sent to Georgetown.

31. At this time it became apparent that there was a serious problem with people who had fled Peoples Temple. Namely, the Parks and Bogue family and Mr. Cordell. These were the individuals who had told me of the possible treachery of Mr. Layton and who stated that they felt themselves, as the first to leave Jonestown, the number one targets of any Jonestown assassins who might still be hunting for them . . . The second problem was the five children lost in the jungle. The families felt they could not leave Port Kaituma without the children or without some word as to their safety . . . I urged each family to leave one male member at Port Kaituma to take care of the children should they be found . . .

32. At about this time, Mr. Jim Cobb emerged from the bush, stating that he had been in the bush ever since he had run there the previous afternoon. He had not seen the other missing persons in the bush. Second Secretary Len Barrett of the Embassy in Georgetown arrived by helicopter from Matthews Ridge to assist with the care of the Americans in what was expected to be the last aircraft of the day for Georgetown. The members of the Parks and Bogue families, Mr. Cordell and Mr. Cobb were flown to Georgetown. (One member of each family remained to search for the children.) Subsequently an aircraft arrived to transport the bodies of Congressman Ryan and the four other dead Americans to Georgetown. Mr. Barrett and I accompanied this aircraft.

Transcript
Jonestown community
November 18, 1978

Peoples Temple members taped the final White Night that Jim Jones held in the pavilion on November 18 shortly after the group with Congressman Ryan left Jonestown for Port Kaituma. Following are notes that may be helpful in understanding the transcript, which reflects the chaos of the events that were taking place.

During the recording, the forty-three-minute tape was stopped and started several times and music was played intermittently.

At the beginning of the transcript, Jim Jones referred to "stolen children" who were with the group that had left Jonestown early that morning under the pretense of going on a picnic. Among the people who were in vehicles headed for Port Kaituma as he now spoke was the father of one of the children.

Jones blamed Timothy Stoen and another member of the Concerned Relatives and Citizens Committee, Deanna Mertle, for instigating Congressman Ryan's trip to Jonestown. Stoen and his wife, Grace Stoen, former members of Peoples Temple, had filed for custody of John Stoen, whom Jim Jones claimed was his biological son. Timothy and Grace Stoen had traveled with Ryan to Guyana and were staying in Georgetown on November 18 with other Concerned Relatives who had not been permitted to travel into Jonestown with Ryan's group. Timothy Stoen was an attorney and represented several former members, including Deanna Mertle and Jim Cobb, in their lawsuits against Peoples Temple.

Deanna Mertle, who changed her name to Jeannie Mills after leaving Peoples Temple in 1975, established the Human Freedom Center in Berkeley, California, which she described as a "halfway house for people leaving cults." She was in the U.S. when this tape was made.

Later on the tape, Jones mentioned former Peoples Temple member Debbie Blakey, who had left Guyana in May 1978. After her return to the U.S., she circulated an affidavit about the possibility of mass suicide in Jonestown. Her brother, Larry Layton, had moved to Jonestown immediately after she left Peoples Temple. In October 1978, their mother, Lisa Layton, had died from cancer in Jonestown.

Jim Jones also reminded the community that the authorities would be after Ujara, Peoples Temple member Don Sly, who had attacked Congressman Ryan with a knife earlier that day.

During his exchanges with a member who protested the taking of their lives and those of the children, Jones alluded to a 1975 movie about Native American Chief Joseph's long struggle to return his tribe to their homelands in *I Will Fight No More Forever, The Story of the Nez Perce Indians.*

Jones also made several references to Richard A. Dwyer, who had already left Jonestown with Ryan's group.

As he relayed the information about Ryan's death to the community, Jones credited the Red Brigade, the Jonestown security team, for "showing them justice."

Near the end of the transcript, Jim Jones mentioned Jim Cobb, one of the "Gang of Eight" who had left Peoples Temple in 1973 and had just been in Jonestown with Congressman Ryan's group to visit relatives. Jim Cobb survived the attack at the Port Kaituma airstrip.

Jim Jones: How very much I've tried my best to give you the good life. But in spite of all of my trying, a handful of our people, with their lies, have made our life impossible. There's no way to detach ourselves from what's happened today. Not only are we in a compound situation, not only are there those who have left and committed the betrayal of the century, some have stolen children from others, and are in pursuit right now to kill them, because they stole their children. We are sitting here waiting on a powder keg. I don't think it is what we want to do with our babies. I don't think that's what we had in mind to do with our babies. It is said by the greatest of prophets from time immemorial, "No man may take my life from me, I lay my life down." So to sit here and wait for the catastrophe that's going to happen on that airplane—it's going to be a catastrophe, it almost happened here. Almost happened—the congressman was nearly killed here. But you can't steal people's children. You can't take off with people's children without expecting a violent reaction. And that's not so unfamiliar to us either, if we were Judeo-Christian—if we weren't Communists. The world *(garbled)* selfish violence, and the violence will take it by force. If we can't live in peace, then let's die in peace. *(Applause)* We've been so betrayed. We have been so terribly betrayed. But we've tried and as Jack Beam often said—I don't know why he said it—I just know Jack, he said—if this only works one day, it was worthwhile. *(Applause)*

Thank you. Now what's going to happen here in a matter of a few minutes is that one of those people on that plane is gonna shoot the pilot. I know that. I didn't plan it, but I know it's going to happen. They're gonna shoot that pilot, and down comes that plane into the jungle. And we had better not have any of our children left when it's over, because they'll parachute in here on us. I'm going to be just as plain as I know how to tell you. I've never lied to you. I never have lied to you. I know that's what's gonna happen. That's what he intends to do, and he will do it. He'll do it. What so being so bewildered with many, many pressures on my brain, seeing all these people behave so treasonous—there was too much for me to put together, but I now know what he was telling me. And it'll happen. If the plane gets in the air even.

So my opinion is that we be kind to children and be kind to seniors and take the potion like they used to take in ancient Greece, and step over quietly, because we are not committing suicide. It's a revolutionary act. We can't go back. They won't leave us alone. They're now going back to tell more lies, which means more congressmen. And there's no way, no way we can survive.

Anybody, anyone who has any dissenting opinion, please speak. Yes. You can have an opportunity, but if our children are left, we're going to have them butchered. We can make a strike, but we'll be striking against people that we—we don't want to strike against. And what we'd like to get are the people that caused this stuff, and some—if some people here are prepared and know how to do that, to go in town and get Timothy Stoen, but there's no plane. There's no plane. You can't catch a plane in time. He's responsible for it. He brought these people to us. He and Deanna Mertle. The people in San Francisco will not be idle over there. They'll not take our death in vain, you know. Yes, Christine.

Christine Miller: Is it too late for Russia?

Jones: Here's why it's too late for Russia. They killed. They started to kill. That's why it makes it too late for Russia. Otherwise I'd say, Russia, you bet your life. But it's too late. I can't control these people. They're out there. They've gone with the guns. And it's too late. And once we kill anybody—at least that's what I've always—I've always put my lot with you. If one of my people do something, it's me. And they say I don't have to take the blame for this, but I can't—I don't live that way. They said deliver up Ujara, who tried to get the man back here. Ujara, whose mother's been lying on him and lying on him and trying to break up this family. And they've all agreed to kill us by any means necessary. You think I'm going to deliver them Ujara? Not on your life.

People: No.

Jones: No.

Ujara: Is there any way that if I go that it'll help us?

Jones: No. You're not going. You're not going.

People: No.

Jones: You're not going. I can't live that way. I cannot live that way. I've lived with—for all, and I'll die for all. *(Applause)* I've been living on a hope for a long time, Christine, and I appreciate—you've always been a very good agitator. I like agitation, because you have to see two sides of one issue, two sides of a question. But what those people are gonna get done, once they get through, will make our lives worse than hell. They'll make us—make the rest of us not accept it. When they get through lying. They posed so many lies between there and that truck that we are done-in as far as any other alternative.

Miller: Well, I say let's make an airlift to Russia. That's what I say. I don't think nothing is impossible if you believe it.

Jones: How are we going to do that? How are you going to airlift to Russia?

Miller: Well, I thought you—they said if we got in an emergency, that they gave you a code to let them know.

Jones: No, they didn't. They gave us a code that they'd let us know on that issue, not us create an issue for them. They said if we—if they saw the country coming down they agreed they'd give us a code. They'd give us a code. We—you can check on that and see if it's on the code. We can check with Russia to see if they'll take us in immediately, otherwise we die. I don't know what else you say to these people. But to me, death is not—death is not a fearful thing. It's living that cuts ya. *(Applause)* I have never, never, never, never seen anything like this before in my life. I've never seen people take the law in their own hands and provoke us and try to purposely agitate murder of children. There is no—Christine, it's just not—it's just not worth living like this. Not worth living like this.

Miller: I think that there were too few who left for twelve hundred people to give them their lives for those people that left.

Jones: Do you know how many left?

Miller: Oh, twenty-odd. That's—That's a small . . .

Jones: Twenty-odd, twenty-odd.

Miller: Compared to what's here.

Jones: Twenty-odd. But what's gonna happen when they don't leave? I hope that they could leave. But what's gonna happen when they don't leave?

Miller: You mean the people here?

Jones: Yeah. What's going to happen to us when they don't leave? When they get on the plane and the plane goes down?

Miller: I don't think they'll do that.

Jones: You don't think they'll go down? I wish I could tell you you were right, but I'm right. There's one man there who blames, and rightfully so, Debbie Blakey for the murder—for the murder of his mother—and he'll stop that pilot by any means necessary. He'll do it. That plane will come out of the air. There's no way you can fly a plane without a pilot.

Miller: I wasn't speaking about that plane. I was speaking about a plane for us to go to Russia . . .

Jones: You think Russia's gonna want us with all this stigma? We had some value, but now we don't have any value.

Miller: Well, I don't see it like that. I mean I feel like that as long as there's life, there's hope. That's my faith.

Jones: Well someday, everybody dies. Someplace that hope runs out, because everybody dies. I haven't seen anybody yet didn't die. And I'd like to choose my own kind of death for a change. I'm tired of being tormented to hell, that's what I'm tired of. Tired of it. *(Applause)* Twelve hundred people's lives in my hands, and I certainly don't want your life in my hands. I'm going to tell you, Christine, without me, life has no meaning. *(Applause)* I'm the best thing you'll ever have. I want, I have to pay—I'm standing with Ujara. I'm standing with those people. They're part of me. I could detach myself. I really could detach myself. No, no, no, no, no, no. I never detach myself from any of your troubles. I've always taken your troubles right on my shoulders. And I'm not going to change that now. It's too late. I've been running too long. Not going to change now. *(Applause)* Maybe the next time you'll get to go to Russia. The next time round. This is—what I'm talking about now is the dispensation of judgment. This is a revolutionary—it's a revolutionary suicide council. I'm not talking about self-destruction. I'm talking about what—we have no other road. I will take your call. We will put it to the Russians. And I can tell you the answer now, because I'm a prophet. Call the Russians and tell them, and see if they'll take us.

Miller: I said I'm not ready to die. But I know—

Jones: I don't think you are. I don't think you are.

Miller: But I look about at the babies and I think they deserve to live, you know?

Jones: I agree. But they—but don't they also deserve much more—they deserve peace.

People: Right.

Miller: We all came here for peace.

Jones: And we've—have we had it?

Miller: No.

Jones: I tried to give it to you. I've laid down my life, practically. I've practically died every day to give you peace. And you still [do] not have any peace. You look better than I've seen you in a long while, but it's still not the kind of peace that I wanted to give you. A person's a fool who continues to say that they're winning when you're losing. Win one, lose two. What? I didn't hear you, ma'am. You'll have to speak up. Ma'am, you'll have to speak up . . . That's a sweet thought. Who said that? Come on up and speak it again, honey. Say what you want to say about *(garbled)* is taking off. No plane is taking off. It's suicide. Plenty have done it. Stoen has done it. But somebody ought to live. Somebody—can they talk to—and I've talked to San Francisco—see that Stoen does not get by with this infamy, with this infamy. He has done the thing he wanted to do—have us destroyed.

Miller: When you—when you—when we destroy ourselves, we're defeated. We let them—the enemies—defeat us.

Jones: Did you see—did you see, *I Will Live to Fight No More Forever?*

Miller: Yes, I saw that.

Jones: Did you not have some sense of pride and victory in that man? Yet he would not subject himself to the will or the whim of people who tell—that they're gonna come in whenever they please and push into our house. Come when they please, take who they want to, talk to who they want to—does this not living? That's not living to me. That's not freedom. That's not the kind of freedom I sought.

Miller: Well, I think where they made their mistake is when they stopped to rest. If they had gone on, they would've made it. But they stopped to rest.

Jim McElvane: Just hold on, sister, just hold on. We have made that day. We made a beautiful day, and let's make it a beautiful day. That's what I say. *(Applause)*

Jones: We will win. We win when we go down. Tim Stoen has nobody else to hate. He has nobody else to hate. Then he'll destroy himself. I'm speaking here not as the administrator. I'm speaking as a prophet today. I wouldn't have set in this seat and talked so serious if I didn't know what I was talking about. Has anybody called back? The immense amount of damage that's going to be done, but I cannot separate myself from the pain of my people. You can't either, Christine, if you stop to think about it. You can't separate yourself. We've walked too long together.

Miller: I well know that. But I still think, as an individual, I have a right to—

Jones: You do, and I'm listening.

Miller:—to say what I think, what I feel. And I think we all have a right to our own destiny as individuals.

Jones: Right.

Miller: And I think I have a right to choose mine, and everybody else has a right to choose theirs.

Jones: Mmm-hmm.

Miller: You know?

Jones: Mmm-hmm. I'm not criticizing—what's that? That's today. That's what 20 people said today. We're alive.

Miller: Well, I think I still have a right to my own opinion.

Jones: I'm not taking it from you. I'm not taking it from you.

McElvane: Christine, you're only standing here because he was here in the first place. So I don't know what you're talking about—having an individual life. Your life has been extended to the day that you're standing there, because of him.

Jones: I guess she has as much right to speak as anybody else, too. What did you say, Ruby? Well, you'll regret that this very day if you don't die. You'll regret it if you do, though you don't die. You'll regret it.

Woman 1: You've saved so many people.

Jones: I've saved them. I saved them, but I made my example. I made my expression. I made my manifestation, and the world was ready—not ready for me. Paul said, "I was a man born out of due season." I've been born out of due season, just like we all are, and the best testimony we can make is to leave this goddamn world. *(Applause)*

Woman 1: You must prepare to die.

Miller: I'm not talking to her. Will you let—would you—would you let her or let me talk?

Jones: Keep talking.

Miller: Would you make her sit down and let me talk while I'm on the floor or let her talk?

Jones: How can you tell the leader what to do if you live? I've listened to you. You asked me about Russia. I'm right now making a call to Russia. What more do you suggest? I'm listening to you. You've got to give me one slight bit of encouragement. I just now instructed her to go there and do that.

McElvane: All right now, everybody hold it. We didn't come—hold it. Hold it. Hold it. Hold it.

Jones: Let *(garbled)* be maintained. *(People speaking)* To lay down your burden. I'm gonna lay down my burden. Down by the riverside. Shall we lay them down here in—by Guyana? What's the difference? No man didn't take our lives. Right now. They haven't taken them. But when they start parachuting out of the air, they'll shoot some of our innocent babies. I'm not lying—I don't wanna *(garbled)*, Christine. But they gotta shoot me to get through to some of these people. I'm not letting them take your child. Can you let them take your child?

People: No, no, no, no.

Woman 2:—gonna die?

Jones: What's that?

Woman 2: You mean you want us to die—

Jones: I want to see—*(People shouting)* Please, please, please, please, please, please, please, please, please, please.

Woman 3: Are you saying that you think we could have smaller blame than other children were?

Jones: John-John—

Woman 3: Because if you're saying—

Jones: Do you think I'd put John's life above others? If I put John's life above others, I wouldn't be standing with Ujara. I'd send John out, and he could go out on the driveway tonight.

Woman 3: Because he's young.

Jones: I know, but he's no different to me than any of these children here. He's just one of my children. I don't prefer one above another. I don't prefer him above Ujara. I can't do that. I can't separate myself from your actions or his actions. If you'd done something wrong, I'd stand with you. If they wanted to come and get you, they'd have to take me.

Man 2: We're all ready to go. If you tell us we have to give our lives now, we're ready—at least the rest of the sisters and brothers are with me.

Jones: Some months I've tried to keep this thing from happening. But I now see it's the will—it's the will of Sovereign Being that this happen to us. That we lay down our lives in protest against what's being done. That we lay down our lives to protest in what's being done. The criminality of people. The cruelty of people. Who walked out of here today? Did you notice who walked out? Mostly white people. Mostly white people walked. I'm so grateful for the ones that didn't—those who knew who they are. I just know that there's no point—there's no point to this. We are born before our time. They won't accept us. And I don't think we should sit here and take any more time for our children to be endangered. Because if they come after our children, and we give them our children, then our children will suffer forever.

Miller: (garbled)

Jones: I have no quarrel with you coming up. I like you. I personally like you very much.

Miller: People get hostile when you try and—

Jones: Oh, well, some people do—but then, you know, yes—yes, some people do. Put it that way—I'm not hostile. You had to be honest, but you've stayed, and if you wanted to run, you'd have run with them 'cause anybody could've run today. What would anyone do? I know you're not a runner. And I would—your life is precious to me. It's as precious as John's . . . What I do, I do with weight and justice and judgment. I've weighed it against all evidence.

Miller: That's all I've got to say.

Jones: What comes now, folks? What comes now?

Man 3: Everybody hold it. Sit down.

Jones: Say it. Say (garbled) What's come. Don't let—take Dwyer on down to the East House. Take Dwyer.

Woman 4: Everybody be quiet, please.

Jones:—got some respect for our lives.

McElvane: That means sit down, sit down. Sit down.

Jones: I know. (Groan) I tried so very, very hard. They're trying over here to see what's going to—what's going to happen in Los Angel—who is it? (People speaking) Get Dwyer out of here before something happens to him. Dwyer? I'm not talking about Ujara. I said Dwyer. Ain't nobody gonna take Ujara. I'm not lettin' 'em take Ujara. Gather in, folks. It's easy. It's easy. Yes, my love.

Woman 5: At one time, I felt just like Christine felt. But after today, I don't feel anything because the biggest majority of people that left here for a fight, and I know, it really hurt my heart because—

Jones: Broke your heart, didn't it?

Woman 5: It broke my heart, to think that all of this year the white people had been with us, and they're not a part of us. So we might as well end it now because I don't see—

Jones: It's all over. The congressman has been murdered. Well, it's all over, all over. What a legacy. What a legacy. What the Red Brigade doin' one bit that made any sense anyway? They invaded our privacy. They came into our home. They followed us six thousand miles away. Red Brigade showed them justice. The congressman's dead. Please get us some medication. It's simple. It's simple. There's no convulsions with it. It's just simple. Just please get it. Before it's too late. The GDF [Guyana Defense Force] will be here, I tell you. Get movin', get movin', get movin'.

Woman 6: Now. Do it now!

Jones: Don't be afraid to die. You'll see, there'll be a few people land out here. They'll torture some of our children here. They'll torture our people. They'll torture our seniors. We cannot have this. Are you going to separate yourself from whoever shot the congressman? I don't know who shot him.

People: No. No. No.

Jones: Just speak their piece. And those who had a right to go, and they had a right to—how many are dead? Aw, God Almighty, God Almighty. Patty Parks is dead?

Woman 7: Some of the others who endure long enough in a safe place to write about the goodness of Jim Jones.

Jones: I don't know how in the world they're ever going to write about us. It's just too late. It's too late. The congressman's dead. The congressman lays dead. Many of our traitors are dead. They're all layin' out there dead. I didn't, but my people did. My people did. They're my people, and they've been provoked too much. They've been provoked too much. What's happened here's been to—basically been an act of provocation.

Woman 8:—want Ted? If there's any way it's possible to have and to give Ted something to take, then I'm satisfied, okay?

Jones: Okay.

Woman 8: I said if there's any way you can do before I have to give Ted something, so he won't have to let him go through okay, and I'm satisfied.

Jones: That's fine. Okay, yes. Yes. Yes.

Woman 9:—and I appreciate you for everything. You are the only—you are the only—you are the only. And I appreciate you—*(Applause)*

Jones: Please, can we hasten? Can we hasten with that medication? You don't know what you've done. And I tried. *(Applause)* They saw it happen and ran into the bush and dropped the machine guns. I never in my life. But *(garbled)* more. But we've got to move. Are you gonna get that medication here? You've got to move. Marceline, in about forty minutes.

Nurse: You have to move, and the people that are standing there in the aisles, go stand in the radio room yard. Everybody get behind the table and back this way, okay? There's nothing to worry about. Every—everybody keep calm and try and keep your children calm. And all those children that help, let the little children in and reassure them. They're not crying from pain. It's just a little bitter tasting. It's not—they're not crying out of any pain. Annie Miguel, can I please see you back—

McElvane:—things I used to do before I came here. So let me tell you about it. It might make a lot of you feel a little more comfortable. Sit down and be quiet, please. One of the things I used to do, I used to be a therapist. And the kind of therapy that I did had to do with reincarnation in past life situations. And every time anybody had the experience of it—of going into a past life, I was fortunate enough through Father to be able to let them experience it all the way through their death, so to speak. And everybody was so happy when they made that step to the other side.

Jones:—to do, but step that way. It's the only way to step. But that choice is not ours now. It's out of our hands. *(Children crying)*

McElvane: If you have a body that's been crippled, suddenly you have the kind of body that you want to have.

Jones: Somebody give them a little rest, a little rest.

McElvane: It feels good. It never felt so good—may I tell you. You've never felt so good as how that feels.

Jones: And I do hope that those attorneys [Charles Garry and Mark Lane] will stay where they belong and don't come up here. What is it? What happened? What is it? They what? All right, it's hard but only at first—only at first is it hard. It's hard only at first. Living—when you're looking at death, it only looks—living is much, much more difficult. Raising up every morning and not knowing what's going to be the night's bringing. It's much more difficult. It's much more difficult. *(People crying and talking)*

Woman 10: I just want to say something for everyone that I see that is standing around and—or crying. This is nothing to cry about. This is something we could all rejoice about. We could be happy about this. They always told us that we could cry when you're coming into this world. So when we're leaving, and we're gonna leave it peaceful, I think we should be—we should be happy about this. I was just thinking about Jim Jones. He just has suffered and suffered and suffered. We have the honor guard, and we don't even have a chance to *(garbled)* got here. I want to give him one more chance. There's just one more thing I want to say. That's few that's gone, but many more here. That's not all of us. That's not all yet. That's just a few that have died. I tried to get to the one that *(garbled)* there's a kid over there—I'm looking at so many people crying. I wish you would not cry. And just thank Father. *(garbled)* been here about *(Applause)* I've been here one year and nine months. And I never felt better in my life. Not in San Francisco, but until I came to Jonestown. I had a very good life. I had a beautiful life. And I don't see nothing that I could be sorry about. We should be happy. At least I am. That's all I'm gonna say. *(Applause)*

Woman 11:—good to be alive today. I just like to thank Dad, 'cause he was the only one that stood up for me when I needed him. And thank you, Dad.

Woman 12: I'm glad you're my brothers and sisters, and I'm glad to be here. Okay.

Jones: Please. For God's sake, let's get on with it. We've lived—we've lived as no other people have lived and loved. We've had as much of this world as you're gonna get. Let's just be done with it. Let's be done with the agony of it. *(Applause)* It's far, far harder to have to walk through every day, die slowly— and from the time you're a child till the time you get gray, you're dying. Dishonest, and I'm sure that they'll—they'll pay for it. They'll pay for it. This is a revolutionary suicide. This is not a self-destructive suicide. So they'll pay for this. They brought this upon us. And they'll pay for that. I leave that destiny to them. Who wants to go with their child has a right to go with their child. I think it's humane. I want to go—I want to see you go, though. They can take me and do what they want—whatever they want to do. I want to see you go. I don't want to see you go through this hell no more. No more, no more, no more. We're trying. If everybody will relax. The best thing you do is to relax, and you will have no problem. You'll have no problem with this thing, if you just relax.

Man 4:—a great deal because it's Jim Jones. And the way the children are laying there now, I'd rather see them lay like that than to see them have to die like the Jews did, which was pitiful anyhow. And I'd just like to thank Dad for giving us life and also death. And I appreciate the fact of the way our children are going. Because, like Dad said, when they come in, what they're gonna do to our children—they're gonna massacre our children. And also the ones that they take captured, they're gonna just let them grow up and be dummies like they want them to be. And not grow up to be a socialist like the one and only Jim Jones. So I'd like to thank Dad for the opportunity for letting Jonestown be, not what it could be, but what Jonestown is. Thank you, Dad. *(Applause)*

Jones: It's not to be afeared. It is not to be feared. It's a friend. It's a friend—sitting there, show your love for one another. Let's get gone. Let's get gone. Let's get gone. *(Children crying)* We had nothing we could do. We can't—we can't separate ourselves from our own people. For twenty years laying in some old rotten nursing home. Taking us through all these anguish years. They took us and put us in chains and that's nothing. This business—that business—there's no comparison to that, to this. They've robbed us of our land, and they've taken us and driven us and we tried to find ourselves. We tried to find a new beginning. But it's too late. You can't separate yourself from your brother and your sister. No way I'm going to do it. I refuse. I don't know who fired the shot. I don't know who killed the congressman. But as far as I am concerned, I killed him. You understand what I'm saying? I killed him. He had no business coming. I told him not to come.

Woman 13: Right, right. *(People crying)*

Jones: I, with respect, die with a degree of dignity. Lay down your life with dignity. Don't lay down with tears and agony. There's nothing to death. It's like Mac [Jim McElvane] said. It's just stepping over into another plane. Don't be this way. Stop this hysterics. This is not the way for people who are socialists or communists to die. No way for us to die. We must die with some dignity. We must die with some dignity. We will have no choice. Now we have some choice. Do you think they're gonna stand—allow this to be done and allow us to get by with this? You must be insane. Look children, it's just something to put you to rest. Oh, God. *(Children crying)* Mother, Mother, Mother, Mother, Mother, please. Mother, please, please, please. Don't—don't do this. Don't do this. Lay down your life with your child. But don't do this.

Woman 14: We're doing all of this for you.

Jones: Free at last. Peace. Keep your emotions down. Keep your emotions down. Children, it will not hurt. If you'll be—if you'll be quiet. If you'll be quiet. *(People crying)* It's never been done before, you say. It's been done by every tribe in history. Every tribe facing annihilation. All the Indians of the Amazon are doing it right now. They refuse to bring any babies into the world. They kill every child that comes into the world, because they don't want to live in this kind of a world. So be patient. Be patient. Death is—I tell you, I don't care how many screams you hear, I don't care how many anguished cries, death is a million times preferable to ten more days of this life. If you knew what was ahead of you—if you knew what was ahead of you, you'd be glad to be stepping over tonight. Death, death, death is common to people. And the Eskimos, they take death in their stride. Let's be dignified. If you'll quit tell them they're dying—if you adults would stop some of this

Entrance sign to Jonestown. "Welcome to Jonestown
Peoples Temple Agricultural Project." May 1978. MSP 3802

Laundry building in Jonestown. May 1978. MSP 3802

Jonestown residents in line for lunch. May 1978. MSP 3802

Jonestown cabins. May 1978. MSP 3802

Peoples Temple members in one of several vehicles that could manage the rough six-mile road between Port Kai-tuma and Jonestown. May 1978. MSP 3802

Dear Phyllis Houston,

Augst 25, 1977

I am in the Freedom land now and I like it very much here. The tree are very beautiful here and our houses are painted different colors. Yesterday I tasted my first peice of sugar cane it is very sweet here and I tasted milo drink it is a drink that taste like choc and marsh. Then last night we had cassav and some very good chicken and some good sweet and sour punch. Down here bananas grow so big you could use them for a year. We have numbers were we live like or our house we have c-5 0-5. The sky is so beautiful at night. Do not bring a coat because you will not need it here.

P.S will you please send me some gum about 6 packs please-por-Favor

Frances
Buckley
Please send the gum

Twelve-year-old Frances Buckley wrote this letter to a Peoples Temple member in San Francisco several days after she arrived in Guyana. MS 3800

Peoples Temple member in Jonestown. MSP 3800

Cuffy Memorial Baby Nursery in Jonestown. Wooden bear-
shaped plaques adorn exterior building walls. FBI

Top: Peoples Temple member in Jonestown. Tommy Johnson, gardening supervisor. MSP 3800
Bottom: Against Jim Jones's wishes, Jonestown residents built a wooden platform basketball court. In November 1978, the Jonestown basketball team played in a tournament with the Guyana National team in Georgetown. FBI

Relatives of Jonestown residents and former members of
Peoples Temple demonstrate in front of Federal Building,
San Francisco, to demand an investigation of Jim Jones.
May 10, 1978. MSP 4062

nonsense. Adults, adults, adults. I call on you to stop this nonsense. I call on you to quit exciting your children, when all they're doing is going to a quiet rest. I call on you to stop this now, if you have any respect at all. Are we black, proud, and socialist, or what are we? Now stop this nonsense. Don't carry this on anymore. You're exciting your children. No, no sorrow that it's all over. I'm glad it's over. Hurry, hurry, my children. Hurry. All I think *(garbled)* from the hands of the enemy. Hurry, my children. Hurry. There are seniors out here that I'm concerned about. Hurry. I don't want to leave my seniors to this mess. Only quickly, quickly, quickly, quickly, quickly. Good knowing you. No more pain now. No more pain, I said. No more pain. Jim Cobb is laying on the airfield dead at this moment. *(Applause)* Remember the Oliver woman said she'd come over and kill me if her son wouldn't stop her? These, these are the people—the peddlers of hate. All we're doing is laying down our life. We're not letting them take our life. We're laying down our life. Peace in their lives. We just want peace.

Man 5: All I would like to say is that my so-called parents are filled with so much hate—

Jones: (Clapping in reprimand) Stop this, stop this, stop this *(garbled)* Stop this crying, all of you.

Man 5:—hate and treachery. I think you people out here should think about how your relatives were and be glad about, that the children are being laid to rest. And all I'd like to say is that I thank Dad for making me strong to stand with it all and make me ready for it. Thank you.

Jones: All they're doing is—all they do is taking a drink. They take it to go to sleep. That's what death is, sleep. I'm tired of it all.

Woman 15: Everything we could have ever done, most loving thing all of us could have done, and it's been a pleasure walking with all of you in this revolutionary struggle. No other way I would rather go to give my life for socialism, communism, and I thank Dad very, very much.

Woman 16: Right. Yes. Dad's love and nursing, goodness and kindness, and he bring us to this land of freedom. His love—his mother was the advance—the advance guard for socialism. And his love and his principles will go on forever unto the fields of—

Jones: Where's the vat, the vat, the vat? Where's the vat with the Green C on it? Bring the vat with the Green C in. Please? Bring it here so the adults can begin.

Woman 16: Go on unto the Zion, and thank you, Dad.

Jones: *(Garbled)* Don't, don't fail to follow my advice. You'll be sorry. You'll be sorry. If we do it, than that they do it. Have trust. You have to step across. We used to think this world was—this world was not our home—well, it sure isn't—we were saying—it sure wasn't. He doesn't want to tell me. All he's doing—if they will tell 'em—assure these kids. Can't some people assure these children of the relaxation of stepping over to the next plane? They set an example for others. We said—one thousand people who said, we don't like the way the world is. Take some. Take our life from us. We laid it down. We got tired. We didn't commit suicide. We committed an act of revolutionary suicide protesting the conditions of an inhumane world.

PART Six

A Community Lost

By November 26, 1978, the world would learn that more than nine hundred people had died in Guyana on November 18, including a mother who killed herself and her three children at Peoples Temple headquarters in Georgetown. It would take weeks for the names of those who died to be available to the public.

The world would also learn that there were survivors. Several journalists, a congressional aide, members of the Concerned Relatives, and the five children who were hiding in the jungle survived the attack on Port Kaituma. Over eighty Peoples Temple members survived in Guyana: members who had left Jonestown before and during the deaths, members who were working in Georgetown or had traveled there for medical care, and members who were on the Peoples Temple's boats.

In San Francisco, Peoples Temple members prepared lists to help identify the dead in Jonestown and filed papers to dissolve the church. The Superior Court of California appointed a receiver to oversee the "dissolution and winding up" of Peoples Temple in January 1979. The receiver arranged to transport 545 bodies from Dover Air Force Base, in Delaware, to the West Coast. He contacted the next of kin and oversaw the burial of the unidentified and unclaimed bodies in Los Angeles and Oakland, California. The last interment service for those who had died in Jonestown was held in June 1979.

The receiver eventually recovered $13 million in assets from the sales of Peoples Temple properties, from accounts in Panama, Caracas, and Grenada, from cash found in Guyana and the United States, and from accrued interest on the funds. Over $1.8 billion in claims were filed against the Peoples Temple estate. Hundreds of claims were filed by people injured at the airstrip, by relatives of the deceased, and by people who had donated their property to Peoples Temple. In 1983, after finalizing settlements with Guyana and the federal government, the court approved payments to individual claimants ranging from $29 to $360,000. The court also approved donations to the Glide Foundation and the San Francisco Council of Churches for their roles in assisting survivors and relatives and agreed to the receiver's request for preservation of the Peoples Temple papers at the California Historical Society.

In 1979 and 1980, U.S. government agencies conducted investigations, held hearings, and issued reports about various aspects of Peoples Temple operations in the U.S. and the death of Congressman Ryan. Trials relating to the deaths in Guyana were held in Guyana and San Francisco. In Guyana in 1980, Larry Layton was acquitted of all murder charges. He was later tried in the U.S. His first trial ended in a hung jury. After the second trial in 1986, Layton was convicted, becoming the only Peoples Temple member to be tried and convicted of conspiring to kill Congressman Ryan and attempting the murder of American Embassy official Richard Dwyer.

The relatives of the people who died on November 18 and survivors of the tragedy were challenged not only by the trauma of the events but also by their inability to obtain information about what had happened in Jonestown, and by the immediate stigma attached to their affiliation with Peoples Temple. A quarter of a century later, unanswered questions about the events, Jim Jones, and the individuals who were lost remain the basis for continued research, investigation, and speculation.

Journal entries
Rebecca Moore
November 19–23, 1978

Rebecca Moore was living in Washington, D.C., when she learned about the deaths in Guyana. She wrote these entries in her journal as she waited for news about her sisters, Annie Moore and Carolyn Layton, and her nephew, Kimo "Jim John" Layton. Her parents, John and Barbara Moore, were living in Reno, Nevada, and had traveled to Guyana to visit their daughters and grandson in Jonestown in May 1978.

In the early news reports of the deaths in Jonestown, there were conflicting and changing stories about the identification of the dead, the death toll, and how people had died. In her November 20 entry, Rebecca Moore noted the news report of the death of Jim Jones, his wife, and young son, fearing the worst: her nephew, Kimo, was a young son of Jim Jones.

19 November

Annie and Carolyn may be dead. A Congressman was shot and killed as he was leaving Jonestown. 4 others killed. No one knows what happened down there, or what is going on now. Reports of mass suicide—but I believe that is untrue, or a set-up, along the lines of Allende's "suicide." If they find people dead someone will already have an excuse.

Today has been spent on the phone, calling Cong. Ryan's office, the State Department, my parents—who were incommunicado all morning. We won't know anything until tomorrow—if then. I am calm, my parents seem calm. We're just waiting for news now. I try not to imagine anything. Just wait. I've re-read Annie's letter to me. I hope she's right; that things will come out before they are all dead.

20 November

I have vacuumed the house thoroughly. The only major chore remaining would be to really clean the kitchen. We went to a movie this afternoon, to get out of the house and numb ourselves.

I can't believe Annie would kill herself. How could Carolyn kill Kimo? It doesn't make sense. If Jim is dead, they probably are also. If he's not—they may have escaped. But where are the missing 700 people who have vanished? Where are they, where are they? It just isn't sinking in. I try to imagine Annie taking poison, helping children take poison. It doesn't fit.

The news media are going ape—much sensationalism, lies, slander, untruths. No one seems to speak for Peoples Temple. No one speaks for the people who have died.

20 November 10 pm

Linda's theory is that some members committed suicide so that others could escape to some kind of hideaway. Only time will tell about that, of course.

The press is going berserk. Stories, accusations get wilder, more vicious, more graphic, lurid. What began as an investigation to see if people were being held against their will became a search for torture and brutality. The news tonight said that a doctor and a nurse administered poison to the people lined up. And that Jim Jones, his wife, and young son (child?) were found dead. I haven't been able to have State Dept. confirm that.

21 November—noon

I told Mom Larry Schacht had administered the poison. She said she knew, but that "Annie wasn't in love with him, he only gave her his guitar." Mom and Dad are incredibly optimistic—they think Annie and Kimo escaped. I don't think so. They're all dead. Even the 700 "escapees" are probably dead somewhere. Why else haven't we heard?

This morning was bad. I clipped articles out of the *Post* and *Star*. Herblock's cartoon: "The Ultimate Cult leader" with picture of the grim reaper . . .

Folks are anxious about the "death squads." I am going to prepare—leave some papers and evidence—in case I am "accidentally" killed in a robbery attempt, or some such bullshit. The FBI is the only "death squad" I know of. And their henchmen, the mafia.

21 November 11:45 p.m.

They've released the first 183 names—Annie and Carolyn are not on the list. What if a miracle happened, what if they aren't dead?

Mom and Dad earlier said they'd pay to have us come out. I told them we'd wait for definite news. They called later to say they wanted us to come (Mom said would we come for Dad's sake; he grumbled; she said, okay, for her sake, too.)

Whenever we see the news—the photos of the bodies lying in embraces, stiff, lying still in the sun, 409 bodies, people—I get chills, shivers.

22 November 1978

Mom is not dealing with things at all. She berates Dad for weeping, and being unable to talk to news reporters. Meanwhile, she busies herself with activity, and surrounds herself with people. She keeps saying that Annie and Carolyn have always come home before. These are delusions.

The papers said that there are paths from Jonestown going to Indian settlements; it is a two-day walk to Venezuela. But the people who fled were those working on the perimeter of the settlement, not the core.

Larry Schacht is dead, Karen Layton is dead, Jim Jones, his wife Marcie. Why shouldn't Carolyn and Annie be dead? And Jim-John? I know they are dead—but when will we hear?

23 November

I talked with Mom and Dad last night. Dad broke down. Mom is very dissociated. She almost broke down, but didn't let herself.

Being here is like being in the twilight zone. Everything is strange, unfamiliar.

Emotions are intense. This morning, Mom and Dad argued. She's afraid Jim is still alive, that Carolyn and Annie are with him in a death squad. The papers said a "female fanatic" with masochistic tendencies was in charge of ordering assassinations. But there was no identification of who that might be.

Last night dad talked about Carolyn, and the chance (fate) that took her to Ukiah, and Peoples Temple. Just chance. He thinks she never resolved her Oedipal feelings. When she was in high school or college she told him she was going to always be a "bachelor girl." And Annie joined Peoples Temple just as she was breaking away from the security of home. Substitutes. Dad said he hoped Annie did not distribute poison, that she did not feed it to babies, children. But if she didn't, if she's not dead, it may be worse.

An awful Thanksgiving. Mom berated us for not mingling with all the guests. She said, to the group, she just worried about Carolyn and Annie's re-entry into society. I said I didn't think she needed to worry about that right now. Dad cried when he said grace. And hugged me. The situation was bizarre. Half of the people were watery-eyed; the other half made jokes. Mom said she was reeling because she'd drunk a lot of wine. The phone rang during dinner—a radio station who wanted to know if Carolyn had been Jim's mistress.

I left several times to go upstairs and just be by myself—second time I managed to sleep awhile. I felt better when I came down. More sociable.

In the living room it was like previous festivities—fun, with good folk and children, jokes, talking, etc. Everyone keeps telling me they're so glad I'm here. I feel torn in two. Dad deals w/things like me; Mom is alienated and oblivious. She doesn't ever cry. It is a strain on their marriage, I think, and that makes me anxious. But I guess I can take some strain off by being here, being a pal to dad. Uncle Bob Moore is coming today, so he will be a man friend for Dad as well. I don't know how to help Mom. She is remote, in her consideration of day-to-day affairs and chores. I feel so bad for her, because it will be worse, the denial and false hopes. It is painful to watch.

from "End Times in Jonestown," in *The Onliest One Alive*
Hyacinth Thrash
Published in 1995, based on interviews from 1983

The Moore family learned that Carolyn, Annie, and Kimo had died in Jim Jones's cabin and that Annie, like Jim Jones, had died from a gunshot wound.

Shabaka Baker and his brothers, Janice Wilsey and her friend Christine Lucientes, Harriet Tropp and her brother Dick, Carol Stahl and her daughter Bonnie, Eugene Chaiken and his family, Marceline Jones and several of her children and grandchildren, Lovie Jean Lucas, Christine Miller, Pop Jackson and his wife Luvenia, Maria Katsaris, John Stoen, Henry Mercer, Cynthia Davis, and Ever Rejoicing, along with hundreds of other Jonestown residents, died that day from cyanide poisoning.

Hyacinth Thrash was one of the survivors. On the morning of November 19, she discovered the deaths in Jonestown when she walked out of her cottage and into a nearby senior dormitory, where she found bodies covered with sheets. Because autopsies were done on only seven of the bodies of those who died in Jonestown, many families would never know with certainty how their relatives had died there.

When the Guyanese soldiers came in, it was about two days after what happened. Stephan Jones, Jim's only natural son, was there. He was saved 'cause he was in Georgetown with the basketball team. Dale Parks and Odell Rhodes was there too. The grounds was covered with reporters. I just said, "No comment." I didn't feel like talking. I was weak, tired, and just wanted to be alone with my thoughts. I was thinking about going back to the States, what my people would think, and all about the people that died. See, I didn't know Ryan was dead and what caused the murders and suicides 'til they found me and told me . . .

After it was all over, I tried not to dwell on it. I was trying to forget. There were all of those dead being put in bags, 913 in all, people I'd known and loved. I wasn't ashamed of what happened, 'cause it wasn't my fault. God knows I never wanted to be there in the first place. I never wanted to go to Guyana to die. I couldn't have prevented it. I wasn't scared either. But I was sorry and hurt. I didn't think Jim would do a thing like that. He let us down . . .

It still worries me, how Zip died. Did she drink the poison?

Letter to Senator John Sparkman, Chairman, Committee on Foreign Relations
James T. McIntyre
December 29, 1978

Immediately following the deaths in Guyana, several U.S. government agencies, including the State Department, the Department of Defense, and the Federal Bureau of Investigation, worked with the Guyanese government to provide security for the sites at Port Kaituma and Jonestown, to remove the bodies from Guyana, to collect Peoples Temple documents to aid in the identifications of the bodies in Jonestown, and to acquire evidence relating to the deaths.

According to a Department of Defense situation report on November 25, 1978, early efforts to identify the bodies in Jonestown were hampered when:

> Tags initially put on bodies by local [Guyanese] officials were prepared utilizing water-soluble ink. Due to the weather conditions, most of this writing became unreadable. Thus the discrepancy between the numbers previous identified and those now being identified. Many of the individuals' clothing are marked with names; however, due to the conditions of the bodies and the relative unreliability of this procedure, markings on clothes was not utilized as a basis for field identification.

The bodies were shipped from Guyana to Dover Air Force Base in Delaware, where government officials immediately embalmed the badly decomposing corpses and continued their efforts to identify them. The costs associated with the U.S. government's transportation, identification, and disposition of the bodies developed into a congressional and media concern as the extent of Peoples Temple financial resources became public.

Dear Mr. Chairman:

This replies to your letter of December 14, 1978, concerning the costs associated with the repatriation of the bodies of American citizens who died at Jonestown, Guyana.

The awful events that occurred in Guyana in mid-November—the assassination of an American Congressman and the suicide-murder of over 900 Americans—are without parallel in American experience. Even now, follow-on actions continue, such as, continued investigations of Federal statutes violated, further identification of the dead and the release of bodies to next-of-kin, and possible suits by the Justice Department regarding the assets of the Peoples Temple organization.

Initially, November 20–21, the Department of State and the U.S. Embassy at Georgetown had agreed upon local burial of the identified remains in Jonestown as the feasible solution to the existence of such a large number of untended bodies. Accordingly, the Embassy advised the Government of Guyana of the U.S. Government's request, in compliance with local law, that interment should begin at once. However, on November 22 the Government of Guyana officially requested the United States to remove the bodies of American citizens at Jonestown and return them to the United States. Apparently, a basic consideration was the Government's fear that the possible flood of next-of-kin wishing to visit the Jonestown burial site and asking for disinterment of bodies of relatives would overtax the Government's transportation and administrative facilities in that part of Guyana. Both our Government and the Government of Guyana were also concerned that facilities were unavailable in Jonestown to identify the dead before burial.

Toward the end of November the Office of Management and Budget, together with the Departments of State and Defense, the Agency for International Development and the other agencies involved, began reviewing the financial aspects of the entire Guyana tragedy, both as to costs and sources of funds.

We have concluded that many of the costs should be considered as part of the normal operations of the agencies . . . The major unusual costs are those of the Defense Department relative to the assistance provided to the Government of Guyana in connection with searching for possible survivors of the tragedy around Jonestown and in complying with the request to remove the dead. Since activities at the Dover Air Force Base mortuary regarding identification and release of bodies are still continuing, the exact amount of the Defense Department costs is not yet known . . .

It is now too early to know whether the legal approaches by the Justice Department regarding the assets of the Peoples Temple organization will result in recoupment of some or all of the U.S. Government's expenses. The Department is pursuing every available approach.

I hope this letter provides you with this information on this subject which you desire.

Sincerely,

James T. McIntyre, Jr.

Director

"The Jonestown Coverup"
from *The Black Panther*
December 16, 1978

The months-long delay in the identification and release of the bodies from Dover Air Force Base prompted the formation of an interfaith Emergency Relief Committee in San Francisco who helped surviving families to obtain their relatives' remains and conducted burial services for the hundreds of unclaimed bodies that were held in Delaware until April 1979. The delay also prompted this December 1978 editorial in *The Black Panther*.

The Jonestown dead must be buried, and they must be buried properly.

Congressman Ryan and the four people who died with him each had funerals. Their bodies were positively identified. It smacks of racism that this government could care less about the identities of the over 900 predominantly Black and poor people who were murdered at Jonestown.

It was not enough for the government to lie and tell us that 900 people living in a new society free of America's oppression committed suicide. Insult has now been added to injury.

First of all, the families of the dead are being told that the bodies of their relatives may *never* be positively identified.

Then, the U.S. military, which sent thousands of young Black and poor men to their deaths in Vietnam, has the audacity to *order* the families not to open the caskets.

Finally grief-stricken mothers and fathers are being told that their loved ones will be cremated in Dover, Delaware, if they cannot come up with $400–$600 (per body) to transport the bodies home.

It makes no difference to the CIA and the FBI that a Black mother may cremate someone else's children besides her own . . .

The callous, blatantly racist treatment given by the government to the grieving families is a further sign of the decadence of American society, a decadence that Peoples Temple has struggled against over the years.

Black and poor people have always had to take care of their own in order to survive in this country, and the present is no exception. We must begin to uncover the truth of the Guyana massacre. If you lost a family member at Jonestown, *demand* that you be allowed to view the body. Don't let anybody tell you that you can't because they will only be trying to cover up their treachery.

from Deposition, *Peoples Temple v. Attorney General of California*

J. Evans

April 4, 1982

On November 18, Jonestown residents sent word to Peoples Temple members in San Francisco that the final White Night was taking place and instructed them to end their lives. Later that evening, members in Georgetown called the San Francisco Temple to contradict those instructions and make sure that they would not kill themselves.

Hundreds of Peoples Temple members in the U.S. survived the deaths in Jonestown.

After providing records to the State Department to help identify the dead and filing court papers to dissolve Peoples Temple, the surviving members faced the challenges of dealing with the deaths of their families and friends and the loss of their homes and community. They strove to establish security and employment in the communities where they hoped to build new lives. But in the wake of revelations in the media about Jim Jones's personal behavior, many employers fired people who they discovered had belonged to Peoples Temple. Survivors struggled with what it meant that they had worked so hard for a group whose tragic end overshadowed all of its accomplishments and the ideals that had led them to become members.

J. Evans left Jonestown with his family on the morning of November 18. In his deposition from 1982, he comments on what it was like to be a member of Peoples Temple before his family's move to Guyana.

I mean, there was a lot of things being said about it, but then put yourself in my place. If you sit there and watch the congressmen and the chief of police and the governor and people like that come to visit a place, you kind of think it's a choice place to be, you know. You consider yourself honored just to be there, you know. Assemblyman Willie Brown was there on several occasions. He made speeches about how the program was an accepted program. I figured if these people—if anybody should know, they should know. You can't be fooling these people.

Then the controversy began. I said anything good people are doing, people are going to talk about it either way. So I kind of compromised with the fact that the good overall would, you know, be more valuable than the bad. I just kind of followed through with that attitude. I can't say I was happy, you know, because I wasn't in it to get the happiness. I was in it to give something, you know. I wasn't there to look at the bad part. I was trying to put in to try to make it build something good.

"Drinking the Kool-Aid"
Michael Carter
November 2003

Michael Carter and his brother, Tim Carter, left Jonestown in the late afternoon of November 18 as Jim Jones was addressing the community in the pavilion. In this essay, Michael Carter took a personal look at the effects of an American idiom that seems disconnected from its tragic origins.

As a surviving former member of People Temple, when I first heard someone speaking about "drinking the Kool-Aid," I was deeply offended. I thought, "How can these people trivialize such a horrific event as the mass suicide/murder of over 900 people?" I thought it, but I didn't say it . . . I have learned it is much easier to keep quiet.

The lessons of life come to all of us, though there are not many who have learned the lessons that those of us in Peoples Temple did. People came to the Temple from different walks of life, but were united in what seemed to be a common cause of racial and economic equality. I was a teenager when I joined Peoples Temple and only twenty years old on November 18, 1978.

I am not a philosopher, but I believe that a person's reaction to my association with Jonestown tells me a lot about what that person's values are. One thing I quickly learned was not to just blurt out at a party or at work that I had lived in Jonestown and survived. People treated me differently after they found out, and usually—okay, always—relationships were affected, colored, tainted by my Jonestown connection. So I adapted and became more selective when sharing my background.

With time I learned. I would let people get to know me for a while, then I would find an appropriate time to let them know that I was in Peoples Temple. They were always amazed, since I was like them. And then, nearly always, even though they knew me, people would distance themselves from me. The knowledge of my background was equivalent to the plague in most cases. Only a few people recognized that if a person like myself—like themselves—was involved in Peoples Temple, then there must be more to the story than what they had heard.

The realization came to me that if I really wanted to represent what Peoples Temple was all about, I had to live my life in a way that reflected the values of Peoples Temple, so if I ever was in a situation where I needed to tell someone that I was in Jonestown, I would properly represent my family that died . . .

Still, it would enrage me when I heard jokes or comments about the "cultists." Arguing and attempting to correct everyone just wouldn't do. What I found truly amazing was the term that I've heard lately in business—"drinking the Kool-Aid"—as a description of someone who has completely bought into a particular idea or belief.

While I was offended the first time I heard the expression, I've thought more deeply about it since. Many of those who died—though certainly not all—did feel they died for what they believed in. If dying for an honorable cause is considered an act of heroism, these people would have been held on pedestals for their bravery and courage . . . if the circumstances of their deaths had been different. Unfortunately, they have been ridiculed and made fun of.

I have had the good fortune to meet a number of wonderful people during my lifetime, but I have never encountered such a concentration of outstanding human beings as I did in Peoples Temple. When I hear "drinking the Kool-Aid," I will continue to remember their dedication for what they believed in. It is easy for people to believe that we were mindless and spineless, but nothing could be further from the truth. I hope someday there will be a few more people who will understand what depths are attached to such a trivial statement.

But trivial or not, I can only imagine how the phrase affects other people who survived Peoples Temple, whether they were in Jonestown or not. I can only speak for myself. I guess I'm still finding ways to survive, to handle the challenges of life that come my way. In the end, that doesn't make me, or any of the other survivors, much different from anyone else.

---

from "The Big Grey"
Tim Carter
November 2003

Tim Carter joined Peoples Temple in 1973. In this excerpt from his writings on his experiences as a member of Peoples Temple and a Jonestown survivor, he focused on how information was withheld—by Jim Jones and fellow members—from the general membership of Peoples Temple.

We were a widely divergent group of human beings committed to an ethos of collectivism. We shared a passionate idealism to make the world a better place. We did not exist in a vacuum. We were a reflection of the economic and political and cultural realities and dynamics of the Civil Rights and Vietnam War generation. Whether one's intentions had been political or spiritual, the Temple seemed to offer the ideal opportunity to effect social change . . .

It is important to understand a crucial dichotomy that exists to this day: what Temple members knew prior to Jonestown and what we have learned (and are still learning) since . . . Much of this new information has come from Temple members themselves who had honored personal vows of secrecy prior to the Temple's demise . . . For example, Peoples Temple had millions of dollars in its bank accounts. Everyone knows that now, but the revelation of it after Jonestown came as a huge shock to me and every other survivor I've talked to . . . That Jones was a drug addict was not known to me or to the vast majority of Temple members. The extent of Jones's sexual abuse of Temple members was far more pervasive than anything I knew or would have imagined . . . The more I learn about Jim Jones and Peoples Temple, the more I am aware of just how much I don't know.

"Jonestown: Frozen in Time"
Melody Ermachild
November 13, 1988

Peoples Temple members were active in all the communities they lived and worked in, especially in San Francisco from 1975 to 1977. After the deaths in Jonestown, many people in the Bay Area found themselves still involved in the Peoples Temple story. Except for the congressional hearings that were held in Washington, D.C., most of the investigations, grand jury hearings, and trials took place in San Francisco. Attorneys, jurors, therapists, social workers, and journalists worked with the many survivors, former members, and relatives who lived in the Bay Area

In her work as a private investigator, Bay Area resident Melody Ermachild interviewed former Peoples Temple members in the United States and traveled to Guyana, where she observed firsthand the remnants of the abandoned agricultural project.

I went to Jonestown two and a half years after the tragedy as one of the handful of lawyers and investigators whose fate it was to document and interpret what happened at Peoples Temple. As a private investigator, it was my job to help explain Jonestown to a jury years later in a San Francisco courtroom.

Our little group flew to Jonestown in a tiny Guyanese government plane. We droned over an endless sea of jungle for an hour, broken on that part of the coast only by the wide surge of the Essiquibo River, which looked like a great muddy lake beneath the plane.

Finally the plane banks sharply over the dirt airstrip, just a brown slash in the ocean of trees, equipped only with a desultory windsock. The broken body of an old plane pushed to the edge of the jungle is the only indication of the purpose of this break in the trees. The airstrip where Congressman Leo Ryan and four others died looks like a rutted muddy road going nowhere.

My work here is to measure and photograph the area and to talk to people who saw the shots fired on that day. Many witnesses are residents of the tiny village of Port Kaituma, who always gathered on the airstrip to see the infrequent arrival of any plane.

And here they are. As we climb down into the hammering sun, a group of ragged village children, tavern denizens, and the constable stand examining our small party. We are obviously Americans, carrying cameras, accompanied by a Guyanese military officer. We can have only one destination: Jonestown, several miles down the road. In spite of the equatorial sun, which intensifies colors, the shadow of Jonestown lies over Kaituma.

The scene looks familiar to me. In a San Francisco office I'd watched hours of videotape of the killings here. I'd seen the old crashed plane, for example, in the background of countless still and moving shots—in slow motion, in freeze-frame, at normal speed: The killers come closer on the tractor-trailer, raise their guns, fire; the cameraman is hit, the camera tilts crazily, the film goes black. The cameraman dies.

Here, the old plane is real. I walk around it. It is the day of the deaths that is irretrievable. Nothing about being here makes that day more understandable. It still feels unreal, incredible, impossible that hundreds of Americans came here, disembarked in Kaituma just as we have, went into the jungle and never went home again.

We have to work fast: we have only one day here. The pilots take off with promises to return for us just before nightfall. We measure, photograph, talk into tape recorders.

Now, unbelievably, a tractor-trailer wheels toward us in the dust. It looks just like the one that carried the shooters who killed Ryan and the others. It may be the same one, but it is simply our transportation to Jonestown. We stand or crouch on its rough wooden cart, bending to duck overhanging branches while it heaves and tosses for more than an hour on the overgrown and rutted road.

First we reach the fields on the edge of Jonestown; after only two years they are overgrown with jungle plants. From a distance the small wooden buildings look normal—maybe a little shabby, unpainted. But as soon as the tractor engine dies it's all wrong, all much too silent. It's a town arrested, baked dead in the relentless heat.

We walk to the "pavilion," a roofed open-air hall where the meetings were held, and where the Flavor-Aid was drunk and injected. This is where Jim Jones held court. Here Jones raved, foul-mouthed and demented. Here the people practiced suicide in the all-night practice drills Jones called White Nights. They practiced several times before the real end came.

Back home, assigned to listen to hours of tapes of Jones' voice, I found I could stand it only in my car, driving the freeways. Maybe, it occurs to me now, that was the closest I could come to the alienation of this environment, where Jones' words fell on human ears.

To my horror, I see nothing has been altered, no one has cleaned up. It is all just as it must have been when the last U.S. helicopter took off with the last of the body bags.

Everywhere lie the people's poor possessions: the worst to see are the shoes, many shoes, cast down as if the feet were a moment ago pulled out of them. They mark where the bodies were. Everywhere in the mind's eye lie the bodies, face down, embracing, slightly swollen, the families arrayed together, the 913 dead.

Jim Jones' chair—"Father's" chair—just a rather silly lawn chair really, lies up-ended under the sign: "Those Who Do Not Remember the Past Are Condemned to Repeat It."

The floor is littered with dozens of pink paper Flavor-Aid packets.

Our little group splits up, rushing to photograph as efficiently as possible. Jonestown is guarded by a small garrison of Guyanese soldiers, eight men isolated here for months at a time. Two accompany me as I shoot slides to show in court at home. Afraid of not finishing before dark, I run from spot to spot, and the two young soldiers run along with me. They are solicitous, carrying some of the heavy camera equipment, warning me of rotten boards in the wooden sidewalks. I realize after a time they are watching me with concern, monitoring my emotional reactions to this horrible place. I wonder about their nights here, regret not bringing them some cigarettes or candy.

We visit the row of tiny, stuffy cabins that each housed up to twenty people. Here in a cabin where elderly people were warehoused lived the old woman I had interviewed in California. The night of the deaths she crawled under her bed and hid while every one of the elders in her room was murdered by injection of cyanide. In the morning she walked out and saw all the bodies. She could find no one alive and so crawled back in her bed, where she stayed for twenty-four hours until the soldiers found her, dehydrated but alive.

Many of the old people were found sitting up or lying in their beds. They had been injected with the poison, then covered with sheets.

I pass the basketball court, actually a wooden platform built above the jungle floor, and I see there is still a remnant of net on the basketball hoop. I think about the Jonestown team, those high-energy young men, mostly black teenagers from San Francisco. Most of them lived because they were in the Guyanese capital for a game. I wonder where they are now.

Reaching Jim Jones' own cabin, a pleasant spot sheltered by trees and blood-red flowers, I stand for a while inside, looking at the wooden bed. I am assaulted by memories of the black-and-white photos I've seen of the people found here. Several were in the bed, embracing, others on the floor. Here died Jones' closest confederates. I've talk to their relatives, whose grief is with me as I sift through the clothing, books, papers in the house. A dresser drawer on the small back porch spills out hypodermic needles.

Working steadily, I operate my cameras automatically while my mind veers to the people I've interviewed who loved these people. I know something about many of the dead, because I've met their families, read their writings. I find myself silently pleading with the dead, too late, not to do it, not to choose to die.

The Jonestown deaths are called a mass suicide, the only one known to human history. It is compared to the tragedy at Masada, a Holy Land hilltop town whose beleaguered defenders of a village killed the women and children and then themselves rather than fall into enemy hands. But Jonestown was not Masada. There was no enemy except in the mind of Jim Jones.

Jonestown was not mainly a mass suicide. Most of the deaths were actually murders. Of the 913, about 250 were elderly people unable to care for themselves. Another 250 were children, either of Jonestown families or entrusted to the Temple for foster care. All of these helpless ones were either made to swallow the cyanide drink or injected with it against their will. Only the able-bodied adults committed suicide by drinking the Flavor-Aid.

The distinction between suicide and murder blurred even here. Those who killed their own children had killed themselves, cutting off all hope forever. Once the babies and the elders were dead, they all had to die. It was a killing, a dying, beyond comprehension.

As if to illustrate, we come to the large cage where the group kept Muggs, their pet chimpanzee. I ask the soldier what happened to Muggs. "They killed him," he replies.

In the course of the investigation and trial, I spent hundreds of hours with former Temple members, both defectors and those who remained loyal to Jones until the very end, but who survived because they were not in Jonestown on November 18. All told me of the heat, the isolation, the brutal hard work in the fields, the sedatives in the food, the punishments and the endless harangue by Jones, whose voice was broadcast into every building in Jonestown day and night. They all told me they had wanted to die. I walk here trying to imagine being told I would never be allowed to leave. It is a thought that sends me running back toward the pavilion and the waiting tractor.

We are silent on the tractor on the way out. As we round a curve two Amerindian women emerge from the thick brush along the road. They are heading home to Port Kaituma after work in their fields. The driver stops for them and they climb onto the crowded cart with their tools, both choosing to sit beside me rather than next to the men, whose looks they avoid. Both women are small, compact, with almost brick-red skin and thick jet-black hair. We exchange shy smiles, but don't talk at first.

Nothing lies back up that road but Jonestown; they know where we have been. I am upset, and feel oddly ashamed under their gaze. Nearing the village, I try to strike up conversation. I say we are from California, and that I was taking pictures back there. When we reach the village and pull up in front of the jailhouse, one woman leaves, but the other stands to talk a moment more. Her head reaches my chin. She wears a long skirt of wrapped fabric. We could not be more different, but women everywhere have something to talk about. I volunteer that I have three children at home, to which she replies: "They killed my son."

Her words are so shocking, at first I don't understand. But she repeats it: "They killed my son." Gesturing behind her, she adds, "They killed my friend's three children."

Behind me, the others in my group shout for me to come. The plane's engine can be heard and night is falling. We will be trapped here overnight if we don't take off immediately, and there are no accommodations for us.

I call back, "But—she says her son died in Jonestown." "Come *on!*" is the shouted reply.

Quickly I ask a few questions. She says her name is Iris Dawson. The Jonestown people started a little store In Kaituma, where she met them. They said her son and her friend's children could go to school in Jonestown. When the deaths happened, they killed the four Guyanese children with the others. "Where is your son's body?" I ask. She says she does not know, that Jonestown was sealed off by soldiers afterwards, and all the bodies were taken away.

There is no more time. We look at each other helplessly. There is so much more to say. I write down her name, saying, "I'm sorry" and good-bye, and run to the plane at the last minute.

The children of Jonestown, I remember, could not be identified because they had not been fingerprinted. They could not be matched to their families, either. And so they were buried together in a mass grave in Oakland. A cemetery owner donated the space after the problem of what to do with the 250 children's bodies seemed unsolvable.

Undoubtedly, this is where Iris Dawson's son lies.

At home, I awoke at 4 a.m. from jet lag. It was Easter morning, the most joyous Christian holiday, celebrating resurrection and rebirth. Without waking my family, I got up and began looking in the yellow pages for cemeteries, hoping to recognize the name I had heard mentioned as the Jonestown burial site. One name sounded familiar, Evergreen Cemetery, and I consulted a map, finding it on a hill in East Oakland.

I think I decided to go there, alone at dawn on a cold, foggy Easter morning, to express in some way the grief I felt.

It took me nearly an hour to find the gravesite. I had almost given up when I reached a steep hillside at the very back of the property and found a solitary marker engraved with the words: "IN MEMORY OF THE VICTIMS OF THE JONESTOWN TRAGEDY, NOV. 18, 1978, JONESTOWN, GUYANA."

Some dead flowers in a plastic cup leaned against the marker. The grass around the marker had grown high. I threw away the old flowers and, kneeling, pulled away the weeds and high grass. One mother tidying up for another, Iris, the farmer, who would never visit this grave.

I wrote her a letter later, describing the bay on the horizon, the eucalyptus trees, the grassy hillside and the marker. I have no idea if she ever got the letter, mailed to her name in the town of Port Kaituma.

My second trip to Guyana, four years later, the rains were so torrential that travel into the Jonestown area was impossible by plane or boat, the only ways to get there. No one I met in Georgetown, the capital, including government officials, had ever heard that Guyanese children died in Jonestown. Nor did they want to know. Whoever did this crime, like all the Jonestown killings, may be dead. Everyone wants to forget.

Peoples Temple Chronology

1955   Jim and Marceline Jones and a small group of parishioners establish
        Peoples Temple, an independent Pentecostal church, in Indianapolis,
        Indiana.

1965   Jones family and more than one hundred Peoples Temple members
        move to Mendocino County, in Northern California.

1969   Peoples Temple builds a new church in Redwood Valley, a small rural
        community eight miles north of Ukiah. Church membership grows to
        three hundred.

1970   Peoples Temple begins holding services in San Francisco and Los Ange-
        les and later opens large churches in both cities.

1973   Recruiting drives in African American communities increase the
        church's membership to over twenty-five hundred. Peoples Temple
        votes to establish an agricultural and rural development mission in
        Guyana, South America.

1974   Members travel to Guyana to secure a location for the mission, estab-
        lish headquarters in Georgetown, Guyana's capital, and begin clearing
        land in the jungle for farming and building.

1976   Peoples Temple officially moves its headquarters from Redwood Valley
        to San Francisco, where members establish dozens of communal resi-
        dences, become active in city politics, and publish their own newspaper,
        Peoples Forum.

1977   Former members and relatives organize the Concerned Relatives
        and Citizens Committee to protest Jim Jones's treatment of church

members. Media coverage of Peoples Temple practices and political activities leads to government investigations of the church's financial and social welfare programs. Hundreds of Peoples Temple members, including Jim Jones, move to Jonestown.

1978   California Congressman Leo J. Ryan organizes a fact-finding mission to Jonestown which ends in tragedy: on November 18, Ryan, three journalists, and a longtime member are killed by Peoples Temple members, more than nine hundred Jonestown residents die from poison, and four members die in Georgetown.

1979   Peoples Temple assets are frozen and placed under the supervision of the San Francisco Superior Court. Congress holds a hearing about the death of Congressman Ryan.

1983   Over $1.8 billion in claims are filed against the Peoples Temple estate. After overseeing the burial of hundreds of unclaimed and unidentified bodies from Jonestown, the court recovers and disburses $13 million in assets. Peoples Temple is dissolved and its records are deposited at the California Historical Society.

1986   Larry Layton is the only Peoples Temple member to be tried and convicted of conspiring to kill Congressman Ryan.

Note on Graphics

Many of the images in *Dear People: Remembering Jonestown* are from the Peoples Temple Collection at the California Historical Society (CHS).

The images where MSP 3800 is noted in the caption are from Peoples Temple records, 1931–1983. Peoples Temple volunteers were the photographers and are not identified in the collection, which includes seven thousand passport photographs, four thousand membership photographs, and twelve hundred candid, publicity, and general images. The photographs of his family and Peoples Temple members that Stephan Jones has shared with CHS are also included in this collection. After settling the estate of Peoples Temple in 1983, Robert Fabian, the court-appointed receiver, donated more than one hundred and thirty cartons of materials to CHS.

Images where MSP 3802 is noted in the caption are from Moore family papers, 1968–1988. John and Barbara Moore took these photographs when they visited their daughters Annie Moore and Carolyn Layton and grandson, Kimo Layton, in Jonestown in May 1978. The Moores donated personal correspondence and papers related to their investigation of the Jonestown tragedy to CHS after the tenth anniversary of the deaths.

Images where MSP 3803 is noted in the caption are from the John R. Hall research materials on Peoples Temple, 1954–1987. Scholar and author John R. Hall originally obtained these photographs of Jonestown from Charles R. Garry, a lawyer who worked for Peoples Temple. The photographers were Peoples Temple members. In 1987, Hall donated his supporting documents for his book *Gone from the Promised Land: Jonestown in American Cultural History* to CHS.

We have included one image in this book from MSP 4062, the Ross E. Case collection pertaining to Peoples Temple, 1961–1984. The photographer is unknown. Case was an associate minister of Peoples Temple from 1961–1963 and participated in the Concerned Relatives and Citizens Committee. CHS received this collection from his wife in 1999.

Although MS 3801, the FBI collection of Peoples Temple papers from Jonestown, Guyana: photocopies, 1972–1978, does not contain photographs, some of the images related to

Jonestown that the FBI holds are available online at *Alternative Considerations of Jonestown and Peoples Temple*, http://jonestown.sdsu.edu/ The photographers were Peoples Temple members. Images where FBI is noted in the caption are accessible from this website and were obtained under the Freedom of Information Act.

Photos appearing inside front and back covers are all from MSP 3800.

Inside front cover:
Row 1: Eva Pugh, Lovie Jean Lucas, Lois Breidenbach, Searcy Darnes
Row 2: Harriet Tropp, Dorrus Soloman, Laketta Franklin, Isabel Davis
Row 3: Claude Goodspeed, Gabriel Dennis, Michaeleen Brady, Alvin Simon Jr.
Row 4: Sharon Kislingbury, Tommy Kice, Denise Johnson, Casandra Lewis
Row 5: Zipporah Edwards, Jose Simon, Corrine Jackson, Eugenia Gernandt

Inside back cover:
Row 1: Ruby Lee Johnson, Earnest Jones, Marceline Jones, Patty McCoy
Row 2: Lynetta Jones, Eliza Jones, Janice Johnson, Shabaka Baker
Row 3: Diana Marshall, Koya Johnson, Eleanor Beam, Don Jackson
Row 4: Geraldine Bailey, Donald Fitch, Janice Wilsey, Dick Tropp
Row 5: Christine Bates, Dawnyelle Fitch, Janet Tupper, Henry Mercer

Sources

"After Guyana–What Could Happen." Editorial. *Oakland Tribune* 22 Nov. 1978: 18.

Baker, Shabaka. Personal History. [1978]. FF-2-95-a, FBI Collection of Peoples Temple Papers from Jonestown. MS 3801, California Historical Society. The Federal Bureau of Investigation (FBI) numbered more than thirty-six thousand pages in this collection. Wherever possible, the number assigned to the document is cited. Many of these records are also available on CD from the FBI under the Freedom of Information Act. http://www.fbi.gov/

Beam, Jack. "History of the Church in California." 27 Sep. 1978. HH8B4, FBI Collection of Peoples Temple Papers. MS 3801, California Historical Society.

Blacken, John. Memo to Secretary of State. 19 April 1977. Folder 176, Moore Family Papers. MS 3802, California Historical Society.

"Blood on the Land of the Waters." Editorial. *Virginian-Pilot* [Norfolk] 21 Nov. 1978.

Brown, J. Mailgram to President Jimmy Carter. 5 Dec. 1978. Folder 1011, Peoples Temple Records. MS 3800, California Historical Society.

Buckley, Frances. Letter to Phyllis Houston. 25 Aug. 1977. Folder 44, Peoples Temple Records. MS 3800, California Historical Society.

Cartmell, Patricia. "No Haloes Please." [1970]. Folder 18, John R. Hall Research Materials. MS 3803, California Historical Society.

Carter, Martin. "I Come from the Nigger Yard." *Poems of Resistance from British Guiana.* London: Lawrence and Wishart, 1954. Excerpt found in PP-8-K-13, FBI Collection of Peoples Temple Papers. MS 3801, California Historical Society.

Carter, Michael. "Drinking the Kool-Aid." Nov. 2003. *Alternative Considerations of Jonestown and Peoples Temple.* 05 Nov. 2004. http://jonestown.sdsu.edu/

Carter, Tim. "The Big Grey." Nov. 2003. *Alternative Considerations of Jonestown and Peoples Temple.* 05 Nov. 2004. http://jonestown.sdsu.edu/

Certificate of Ordination. 2 Feb. 1956. BB-17-cc, FBI Collection of Peoples Temple Papers. MS 3801, California Historical Society.

Chaiken, Eugene. Letter to Jim Jones. [1978]. BB-10-j, FBI Collection of Peoples Temple Papers. MS 3801, California Historical Society.

———. "Memo: S/M–The U.S.S.R.–Possible Settlement Locations, Geography and

Climate." 25 Oct. 1978. GG-1-c1, FBI Collection of Peoples Temple Papers. MS 3801, California Historical Society.

"Chimp in the Valley." *Temple Reporter* Summer 1973. Folder 1209, Peoples Temple Records. MS 3800, California Historical Society.

Church Bulletin. 1972. Folder 1206, Peoples Temple Records. MS 3800, California Historical Society.

Davis, Cynthia. Personal History. [1978]. FF-2-103-a, FBI Collection of Peoples Temple Papers. MS 3801, California Historical Society.

"Death in Guyana." Editorial. *Sacramento Bee* 21 Nov. 1978.

Dwyer, Richard A. Memo to Secretary of State. 22 Nov. 1978. Folder 2317, Peoples Temple Records. MS 3800, California Historical Society.

Edwards, Zipporah. Letter to Jim Jones. n.d. EE-1E-10-b, FBI Collection of Peoples Temple Papers. MS 3801, California Historical Society.

Ermachild, Melody. "Jonestown: Frozen in Time." *San Francisco Chronicle* 13 Nov. 1988, sec. This World: 10+.

Evans, J. Deposition. 4 Apr. 1982. *Peoples Temple v. Attorney General.* No. 746 571. Superior Ct. of CA. 1983. Folder 2039, Peoples Temple Records. MS 3800, California Historical Society.

"Family Good News." 23 Jan. 1974. Folder 1203, Peoples Temple Records. MS 3800, California Historical Society.

"Followup Notes from Peoples Rally." 8 Aug. 1978. C-8-a-22a, FBI Collection of Peoples Temple Papers. MS 3801, California Historical Society.

Gallup, George Horace. *The Gallup Poll: Public Opinion,* 1978. Wilmington: Scholarly Resources, 1979.

Gang of Eight. Letter to Jim Jones. [1973]. Folder 72, Moore Family Papers, 1968-1988. MS 3802, California Historical Society.

Garry, Charles R. Transcript. 14 Sep. 1978. Folder 10, John R. Hall Research Materials. MS 3803, California Historical Society.

Graham, Billy. "Billy Graham, on the Devil in Mr. Jones." *New York Times* 5 Dec. 1978: A23.

"Guide for the Hostess." n.d. Folder 1024, Peoples Temple Records. MS 3800, California Historical Society.

"Guyana Horror Story." Editorial. *New York Post* 21 Nov. 1978.

"Instructions from JJ." 17 Mar–25 May 1978. EE-1-S-47, FBI Collection of Peoples Temple Papers. MS 3801, California Historical Society.

Jackson, David Betts. "Settin' around Here Free This Morning." [1978]. FF-2-94, FBI Collection of Peoples Temple Papers. MS 3801, California Historical Society.

"Jim Jones Miracle Crusade." 1973. Folder 1203, Peoples Temple Records, MS 3800, California Historical Society.

"Jones and the Politicians." Editorial. *San Francisco Examiner* 22 Nov. 1978: 30.

Jones, James W. "As a Man Thinketh, So He Is." *Herald of Faith* May 1956:1+. Article found in Folder 7, John R. Hall Research Materials. MS 3803, California Historical Society.

———. "Jim's Commentary about Himself." [1977?]. O1-A1-a, FBI Collection of Peoples

Temple Papers. MS 3801, California Historical Society. Another version of this transcript is available from U.S. FBI Peoples Temple Recording, Audiotape Q 134. Transcribed by Fielding M. McGehee III. Jonestown Institute, "Alternative Considerations of Jonestown and Peoples Temple." 05 Nov. 2004. http://jonestown.sdsu.edu/

———. "Reading and Commentary of the News Today." 9-10 Nov. 1978. U.S. FBI Peoples Temple Recording, Audiotape Q 323. Transcribed by Fielding M. McGehee III. Jonestown Institute, *Alternative Considerations of Jonestown and Peoples Temple.* 05 Nov. 2004. http://jonestown.sdsu.edu/

———. Sermon. [c. 1973]. U.S. FBI Peoples Temple Recording, Audiotape Q 929. Transcribed by Fielding M. McGehee III. Jonestown Institute, *Alternative Considerations of Jonestown and Peoples Temple.* 05 Nov. 2004 http://jonestown.sdsu.edu/

———. Sermon. [c. 1973?]. U.S. FBI Peoples Temple Recording, Audiotape Q 162. Transcribed by Fielding M. McGehee III. Jonestown Institute, *Alternative Considerations of Jonestown and Peoples Temple.* 05 Nov. 2004. http://jonestown.sdsu.edu/

———. "Who Are the Real Radicals?" Oct. 1970. Folder 1203, Peoples Temple Records. MS 3800, California Historical Society.

Jones, Marceline. Holographic Will. 25 May 1974. BB-18-J-1, FBI Collection of Peoples Temple Papers. MS 3801, California Historical Society.

———. "Jim Jones as Seen through the Eyes of Those He Loved." n.d. BB-iB-z-69, FF-1-95d, FBI Collection of Peoples Temple Papers. MS 3801, California Historical Society.

———. Letter to Jim Jones. 8 June 1970. BB-18-L-1, FBI Collection of Peoples Temple Papers. MS 3801, California Historical Society.

———. Letter to Jim Jones. 15 Aug. 1977. EE-1-I&J-69, FBI Collection of Peoples Temple Papers. MS 3801, California Historical Society.

———. Letter to Jim Jones. 15 May 1978. N-1-C-31-a, FBI Collection of Peoples Temple Papers. MS 3801, California Historical Society.

———. Letter to Lynetta Jones. 27 Sep 1954. Folder 15, John R. Hall Research Materials. MS 3803, California Historical Society.

———. Memo to Jim Jones. n.d. EE-1-I & J-57, FBI Collection of Peoples Temple Papers. MS 3801, California Historical Society.

Jones, Stephan. "We All Made the Move." [1978]. FF-1-106-c, FBI Collection of Peoples Temple Papers. MS 3801, California Historical Society.

"Jonestown." Editorial. *Birmingham Post* [United Kingdom] 21 Nov. 1978.

"The Jonestown Coverup." Editorial. *Black Panther* [Oakland] 16–29 Dec. 1978: 2.

Jonestown Transcript. 18 Nov. 1978. U.S. FBI Peoples Temple Recording, Audiotape Q 042. Transcribed by Fielding M. McGehee III. Jonestown Institute, *Alternative Considerations of Jonestown and Peoples Temple.* 05 Nov. 2004. http://jonestown.sdsu.edu/

Katsaris, Maria. Letters to Jim Randolph. [1977?]. Folder 1015, Peoples Temple Records. MS 3800, California Historical Society.

"Last Words." 18 Nov. 1978. X-1-a-54, FBI Collection of Peoples Temple Papers. MS 3801,

California Historical Society. The handwriting of "Last Words," an unsigned document, matches that of Peoples Temple member Dick Tropp when compared to samples of his handwriting in the collection.

Layton, Carolyn. "Analysis of Future Prospects." [1978]. X-3-e-32-a, FBI Collection of Peoples Temple Papers. MS 3801, California Historical Society.

Letter to Compatriot Don. Folder 39, Peoples Temple Records. MS 3800, California Historical Society.

Lucas, Lovie Jean. Two Notes. [1978]. PP-15-e-1, FBI Collection of Peoples Temple Papers. MS 3801, California Historical Society.

Lucientes, Christine Renee. Personal History. [1978]. FF-2-93A, FBI Collection of Peoples Temple Papers. MS 3801, California Historical Society.

McIntyre, Jr., James T. Letter to Senator John Sparkman. 29 Dec. 1978. Folder 2388, Peoples Temple Records. MS 3800, California Historical Society.

Mercer, Henry. Personal History. [1978]. FF-2-97-A, FBI Collection of Peoples Temple Papers. MS 3801, California Historical Society.

"A Message in Massacre." Editorial. *San Diego Union* 22 Nov. 1978.

Miller, Christine. Letter. [1978]. EE-2-l-5-A, FBI Collection of Peoples Temple Papers. MS 3801, California Historical Society.

Moore, Annie. Personal History. [1978]. FF-2-98-A, FBI Collection of Peoples Temple Papers. MS 3801, California Historical Society.

Moore, Rebecca. Journal. 19–23 Nov. 1978. Folder 29, Moore Family Papers. MS 3802, California Historical Society. Excerpts from the journal were also published in Rebecca Moore, *The Jonestown Letters: Correspondence of the Moore Family 1970–1985*. Studies in American Religion, vol. 23. Lewiston, NY: Edwin Mellen Press, 1986.

Novak, Michael. "Jonestown: Socialism at Work." *Washington Star* 17 Dec. 1978.

"Peoples Temple Show: A Success." *Guyana Chronicle*. 14 April 1978. Folder 1205, Peoples Temple Records. MS 3800, California Historical Society.

Poindexter, Amanda (Ever Rejoicing). [1978]. Personal History. [FF-2], FBI Collection of Peoples Temple Papers. MS 3801, California Historical Society.

"Resolution of the Community." 9 Nov. 1978. Folder 164, Moore Family Papers. MS 3802, California Historical Society.

Ryan, Leo J. Letter to Jim Jones. 1 Nov. 1978. AA-1-L, FBI Collection of Peoples Temple Papers. MS 3801, California Historical Society.

Smith, J. Alfred. "Breaking the Silence: Reflections of a Black Pastor." *Peoples Temple and Black Religion in America*. Ed. Rebecca Moore, Anthony B. Pinn and Mary R. Sawyer. Bloomington: Indiana University Press, 2004. 139-157.

Stahl, Carol. Personal History. [1978]. FF-1-96 a, FBI Collection of Peoples Temple Papers. MS 3801, California Historical Society.

Thrash, Catherine (Hyacinth), as told to Marian K. Towne. *The Onliest One Alive: Surviving Jonestown, Guyana*. Indianapolis: M Towne, 1995.

"The Tragedy and the Challenge." Editorial. *Sun Reporter* [San Francisco] 23 Nov. 1978: 7.

"This Nightmare Is Taking Place Right Now." May 1978. Folder 66, Moore Family Papers. MS 3802, California Historical Society.

Tropp, Harriet S. Memo to Jim Jones. n.d. FF-5-r-3, FBI Collection of Peoples Temple Papers. MS 3801, California Historical Society.

———. Memo to Jim Jones. [1978]. EE-2-s-13A, FBI Collection of Peoples Temple Papers. MS 3801, California Historical Society.

Tropp, Richard. Personal History. [1978]. [FF-2], FBI Collection of Peoples Temple Papers. MS 3801, California Historical Society.

———. "Who are the People of Jonestown?" n.d. EE-1-T-57, FBI Collection of Peoples Temple Papers. MS 3801, California Historical Society.

U.S. Dept. of Defense. Joint Task Force in Jonestown Situation Report Number Four Part F. 25 Nov. 1978. Folder 117, Moore Family Papers. MS 3802, California Historical Society.

U.S. Dept. of State. "Information Sheet Number 2," and "Information Sheet Number 3." 28 Feb. 1978. MM-8-28, FBI Collection of Peoples Temple Papers. MS 3801, California Historical Society.

"Victims of Conspiracy." [1978]. Folder 38, Moore Family Papers. MS 3802, California Historical Society.

Washington, Huel. "Looking Back on Jonestown: The Real Culprit Is America." *Sun Reporter* [San Francisco] 30 Nov. 1978: 6.

Washington, Vera. "Reflections on Leaving the Temple." Nov. 2003. *Alternative Considerations of Jonestown and Peoples Temple.* 05 Nov. 2004. http://jonestown.sdsu.edu/

Will, George F. "Wild Religions." *Washington Post* 26 Nov. 1978: C7.

Wilsey, Janice. Personal History. [1978]. FF-2-99A, FBI Collection of Peoples Temple. MS 3801, California Historical Society.

Wings of Deliverance. Bylaws. 15 Mar. 1955. Folder 1, Peoples Temple Records. MS 3800, California Historical Society. The founding members of Peoples Temple first called their church Wings of Deliverance. They soon changed it to Peoples Temple.

About the Editor

Denice Stephenson is a special project archivist for the Peoples Temple Collection at the California Historical Society. Since 2000, she has provided assistance to researchers for family, scholarly, and media projects related to Jonestown and Peoples Temple. She lives in San Francisco.